the
MULES
that ANGELS
ride

Other books by Clifford Goldstein:

1844 Made Simple
Between the Lamb and the Lion
By His Stripes
Children of the Promise
The Clifford Goldstein Story
Day of the Dragon
The Day Evil Dies
God, Gödel, and Grace
Graffiti in the Holy of Holies
The Great Compromise
How Dare You Judge Us, God?
Like a Fire in My Bones
A Pause for Peace
The Remnant
One Nation Under God
False Balances
The Saving of America

To order, call 1-800-765-6955.

Visit us at www.reviewandherald.com for information on
other Review and Herald® products.

CLIFFORD GOLDSTEIN

the MULES that ANGELS ride

REVIEW AND HERALD® PUBLISHING ASSOCIATION
HAGERSTOWN, MD 21740

The author assumes full responsibility for the accuracy of all facts and quotations as cited in this book.

Scripture quotations marked NASB are from the *New American Standard Bible,* copyright © 1960, 1962, 1963, 1968, 1971, 1972, 1973, 1975, 1977, 1994, by The Lockman Foundation. Used by permission.

Texts credited to NIV are from the *Holy Bible, New International Version.* Copyright © 1973, 1978, 1984, International Bible Society. Used by permission of Zondervan Bible Publishers.

Texts credited to NKJV are from the New King James Version. Copyright © 1979, 1980, 1982 by Thomas Nelson, Inc. Used by permission. All rights reserved.

Bible texts credited to Phillips are from J. B. Phillips: *The New Testament in Modern English,* Revised Edition. © J. B. Phillips 1958, 1960, 1972. Used by permission of Macmillan Publishing Co.

Bible texts credited to RSV are from the Revised Standard Version of the Bible, copyright © 1946, 1952, 1971, by the Division of Christian Education of the National Council of the Churches of Christ in the U.S.A. Used by permission.

This book was
Edited by Clifford Goldstein
Cover designed by Trent Truman
Interior designed by Candy Harvey
Electronic makeup by Shirley M. Bolivar
Typeset: 11/14 Bembo

PRINTED IN U.S.A.

09 08 07 06 05   5 4 3 2 1

R&H Cataloging Service
Goldstein, Clifford Ralph, 1955-
    The mules that angels ride: provocative essays to affirm your faith and nourish your spirit

—Religious life
1. Seventh-day Adventists   I. Title

286.732

ISBN 0-8280-1914-2

To my dad

CONTENTS

INTRODUCTION

MY ONE PAGE A MONTH

"For unto whomsoever much is given," said Jesus, "of him shall be much required" (Luke 12:48). Scary words, at least for me, considering all that I have been given, which—among other things—includes a monthly column in the *Adventist Review*.

It's a privilege, having been given this column, which is why one thought pervades my thinking in regards to it: *What can I put there that will affirm the faith of those who are reading it?* However varied the topics, or different my styles or approaches, a common thread runs through my one page a month, and that is—to affirm our people in what we believe.

It's simple, really: After 25 years as an Adventist I still believe in this church, its mission, its message, its calling. I believe that God has raised up this body to preach the three angels' messages to the world; I believe that we're the remnant depicted in Bible prophecy; and I believe that—whatever the unexpected surprises—final events will unfold around the issues in Revelation 13 and 14 pretty much as we have been interpreting those chapters for more than a century. Meanwhile the sanctuary, the Sabbath, the state of the dead, the Second Coming, the Spirit of Prophecy—all the teachings we hold as Adventists—form what I believe is "present truth." At the center, of course, is the gospel—the righteousness of Jesus credited to us as our surety of salvation. All these things, and more, I have tried to affirm again and again in my column, hoping that my conviction about these truths will rub off on others.

Yet my motives aren't totally altruistic. I've discovered that, by affirming others, I myself get affirmed. I'm sure, though, that the editors of the *Adventist Review* wouldn't give that one page a month for my own personal edification. Thus, I live with the prayer that my page might do for others what it often does for me.

The *Mules That Angels Ride* is that page, starting back in 1996 (when it first appeared), multiplied down through the years. Though under no illusions that each column will touch everyone, I hope some will reach people just where they had to be reached—and when. If not, the page is a waste of dead tree.

The first section is composed of personal stories of how God worked in my life at various times, setting the background (kind of) for what follows. The next section deals with the big picture, the great controversy scenario in which we and the whole universe are involved. I then get into questions of faith, of why we believe what we do. That naturally leads into my favorite topic, the gospel of Jesus and how God saves us. Once some of these fundamentals are taken care of, we go into a section on prophecy, followed by columns on science and faith, then on issues regarding our church, and concluding with religious liberty. In the whole flow, you'll get a smattering of philosophy, science, literature, poetry, math, and history; that is, generally, whatever I happen to be reading at the time usually winds up, in one way or another, in what I am writing at the time.

It will be obvious, from the start, that the columns aren't neatly divided; some in one section could easily fit into another. Wherever they are, each represents my attempt to express the wonderful truths entrusted to our church. Having been given much, I have tried—with my one page a month—to return what was, as Jesus said, "required."

Thank God, Christ's righteousness covers it all. It'll have to.

City Lights

THIS SECTION COVERS, however sporadically, my own personal journey of faith. It begins in a pizza parlor in Gainesville, Florida, where it first struck me that Truth, as in capital "T," had to exist, a rather startling revelation for a hard-nosed 21-year-old who believed only in what he didn't believe; it ends with me looking back at what was, at the time the column was written, my twentieth year at the General Conference. Sandwiched in between are accounts of some wild various adventures, everything from how I almost got clubbed in a riot in Switzerland to when I almost got fired for allowing a bunch of dissents to stay at my apartment during an Annual Council. Amid the excitement, hilarity, and insanity sometimes depicted here, I still always sought to reveal the mercy and grace of God, who loves us despite ourselves. He'd have to.

Pizza Epiphany

However unintentionally (maybe), my parents—when done raising me—had raised an unrepentant postmodernist. For me, if the same object meant different things to different subjects (one's unclean beast is another's pork chops), then objects meant nothing in and of themselves, but assumed meaning only when subjects attributed meaning to them. Truth was, therefore, subjective; it existed only in the mind, and because different minds saw the same thing differently, objective truth was no more real than the ghost of King Lear's grandfather.

I once hammered this point home to a drunken British Army deserter as we argued about an empty beer bottle in a Stockholm apartment.

"Look," I said, pointing to hollow glass on the table between us. "When you look at that beer bottle, you're seeing something different than I am. You're seeing it from your own angle, which is different from mine. You're seeing it through your own eyes, which see differently than mine do. And whatever you see, you then filter it, interpret it, and emote about it through your own past experiences, which are different from mine. Though we're looking at the same object, how could we possibly see the same thing?"

My epistemological dogmatism was shattered, however, a year later in a Florida restaurant one night when, because of a pizza, I suddenly knew that objective truth *had* to exist. Looking at the meal, I realized that maybe someone believed aliens from the constellation Canis Minor dropped it out of a spaceship; or maybe some subject believed that the pizza arose out of a vicious evolutionary struggle for existence. Fifty people might have been so sure the god Marduk created the pizza that they would not only die, but kill, for this conviction. A million subjects might have held a million different beliefs about the pizza's origins, and maybe every one of them was wrong. But somewhere (even if no human could know where) an explanation about the origin and purpose of the pizza had to exist, and that explanation, whatever it was, was the truth about the pizza.

Then it hit me: just as the pizza had to have an explanation (and whatever that explanation was, it was the truth about the pizza), humanity, the world, and my existence also had to have an explanation (and that explanation, whatever it was, was the truth about the world).

I could hear the racket: 21 years of scaffolding and edifice crashing around me (a personal Copernican revolution is noisy). The epistemological center of gravity was wrenched away from me to a reality that existed outside my mind. Transcending the relativity, subjectivity, and contingency that hijack every human experience, objective reality—originating in something—had to exist. Which meant, then, that truth had to as well. Heresy had become orthodoxy over a pizza.

As I walked outside (the ground feeling harder than ever before) and erratic shadows confused the night, this thought burned inside me: *If it were possible to know this truth about my origins, about my existence, then I wanted to know it no matter where it led me, what it cost me, what I had to suffer, what I had to give up. If I could ever know it, I wanted to know it—no matter what.*

And all I know is this: Two years later, of all the different ways I could have gone, all the different paths I could have taken, I (who hated Christians and vegetarians) ended up becoming, of all things, a Seventh-day Adventist.

Since then I've met those who've said their desire for truth led them *away* from the Adventist Church; or that in their quest for truth they found Islam, or Buddhism, or atheism. Fine—but all these testimonies mean nothing to me personally, because I don't know their hearts and don't have to answer for them. The only one I know, and have to answer for, is my own; and in its painful desire for truth, no matter the cost (which turned out to be, at the time, expensive), I was thrust into the Adventist Church, and nowhere else.

And *that's* the absolute truth.

-∽-

Remembrance of Things Past

I've told my conversion story so often that at times I've thought I'd choke if I told it again. However, after praying, "Lord, as long as it can do some good, I'll keep telling it," I realized that it does good—if for no one but myself. Because it doesn't hurt for me to remember, again and again, how the Lord has worked in my life.

In 1979 I was 23 years old. I had just returned to Gainesville, Florida, after more than a year in Israel and Europe. Having had some amazing experiences, I came to believe in God, or at least in some supernatural transcendence—a radical shift for someone who had always believed that all reality, from dreams to collapsing stars, had only a naturalist, materialistic explanation.

No longer—especially after being swept into the occult. I would lie on my bed when this strange tingling would roll up my body, and I'd feel as if I were hurtling through a wind tunnel. However frightening the experiences, I told myself that the next time it happened, I wouldn't fight it. Sure enough, one afternoon, the sensation moved up my body, centered in my head, and suddenly I shot out of my body, went through the ceiling, and was floating in a gray diaphanous mist outside an apartment of two friends.

Now, please: I am an Adventist *today,* I understand today that there's no such thing as a separate immortal soul, but back then no one could have convinced me that this was anything other than my soul leaving my body.

I had a Bible back then and tried reading it, but I couldn't get past the talking snake. In contrast, after these experiences, I thought that maybe in the occult, in spiritualism, was the truth I had always been seeking, so I was going to study it. On my way to the library I stopped at a health food store. When I mentioned to the owner where I was going (to the library) and why (to delve into the occult), he warned me about the devil (which was like warning me that Santa wouldn't come down the chimney if I were bad). Laughing him off, I nevertheless did take a book he gave me.

I then went into the library, found a book about the occult, and started reading it. After reading a bit, I went to put the book back on the shelf. As I walked through the library, I had in one hand, for the first time in my life, a book on the occult; in my other hand I had, for the first time in my life, the book the owner of the health food store gave me.

Which book was it?

The Great Controversy, of course.

I had, at that time, no inkling about the forces converging on me. Then a few days afterward, Christ converted me, and immediately those occult experiences stopped. Only later did I realize how precariously balanced on the edge I had been, having an occult book in one hand and *The Great Controversy* in the other—both for the first time ever!

Since then I've read about those who have "died" and come back to life, recounting the same kind of experiences I had, only I wasn't near dead. All these, I'm convinced, are supernatural hallucinations by Satan; none of us ever left our bodies. It's all deception, and I shudder when I think how close I came to being swallowed up in it.

Satan, though, with his mind-bending deception, overplayed his hand on this once-hard-core naturalist. When we talk about the devil, we're not talking poetry, allegory, even theology; we're talking about a cunning supernatural entity with the power to control any mind not surrendered to Christ. I know, because I've been there.

Every time I recount this story, that point comes back to me. And, maybe, that's why the Lord has me tell it, again and again . . .

~

When the Nets Are Full

Next to my computer screen the photo stands, squared in wood, flat as glass, a black-and-white print browned by 70 years of air. It's of five men at a desk. One is my grandfather, working as a writer and editor. Just like his brothers; just like his son, my uncle, whose books (unlike mine) get reviewed in the Washington *Post.*

I got it—the writing, the editing—honestly (obviously). Once passing the policeman/cowboy/jet fighter pilot stage, I wanted to be a novelist or nothing. Though not a particularly outstanding high school student, I did OK in English; my teachers sometimes thought I had plagiarized essays (*"You* didn't really write that, did you?").

In my junior year at college a freshman who had been picking illegal mushrooms was, after being handcuffed, shot dead by a cop. For everyone else it was a cold-blooded killing; for me it was the genesis of a novel that unfurled into the story of a relationship between a 17-year-old boy and a

7-year-old girl traveling through Europe together. I even spent time volunteering at an elementary school, just to be around kids so I could make my imaginary one as real as possible.

The book controlled my life more than I controlled the lives in it. Everything external—friends, family, finances—was interpreted, qualified, and analyzed through the template of how they would impact my writing the novel. The book became who I was; I didn't exist apart from it, at least not much of me.

One early evening in the late summer of 1979 I wandered back to my room (in Gainesville, Florida) to continue writing. I had, at this point, poured two and a half years into the novel, more than 10 percent of my life (I was 23), and that evening I felt more excited about the project than ever before. Never had it been going better.

In the room I stuck a sheet of paper in the typewriter, and when I struck the first key—as real as anything that ever happened to me, the Spirit of the Lord Jesus came and said, "Cliff, you have been playing with Me long enough. If you want Me tonight, burn the book."

Now, this didn't happen in a vacuum; the Lord had long been working to bring me to this moment, in which He showed me that the book was my god, and if I wanted the true God, the false one had to go. *But why tonight, when I was more enthusiastic about the book than ever? Why couldn't the Lord have asked me to do this at a time when it wasn't going too well?*

After a night of wrestling, I burned the novel and went to bed amid a cloud of smoke (I had burned it in my room).

As I entered the whole new existence of being born again, the devil within days whispered in the ears of this new believer, full of questions and doubts, *Oh, you burned the book because you needed an excuse to get out because you knew you couldn't do it.* The words stopped me in my tracks; a fearful wave of doubt swept through me. But then, as I recounted the experience of that night, I said, No! No! No! On the contrary, I was never more sure of the book than I was that night—and that's why the Lord had me burn it then! *Get thee behind me, Satan!*

Ellen White (as usual) explains so much: "At the moment of success, when the nets were filled with fish, and the impulses of the old life were strongest, Jesus asked the disciples at the sea to leave all for the work of the gospel. So every soul is tested as to whether the desire for temporal good or for fellowship with Christ is strongest" (*The Desire of Ages,* p. 273).

No fooling.

But, by uprooting us from the world when our roots are the deepest in the world, the Lord makes it more difficult (though not impossible) for those roots to take hold again. We have to commit ourselves at the lowest common denominator of ourselves; otherwise, it's no commitment, only a handshake with our fingers crossed.

-∾-

And the Moral
of the Story Is . . .

Did you ever have something incredible happen, only to forget about it until, thinking about the incident later, you wonder why it didn't make more of an impression on you at the time?

Well, this is one of those experiences. . . .

It was the late summer/early fall 1980. I was working with Hungarian Seventh-day Adventist wall-paper hangers in Switzerland (how I got involved with Hungarian Seventh-day Adventist wall-paper hangers in Switzerland is another story).

Less than a year earlier (at 23), my life had been turned upside down and inside out by having met Jesus Christ. Changing from a secular Jew to a born-again Seventh-day Adventist was a back-breaking transition. It was not easy having almost everything I believed, every first principle, every axiom, every assumption, shown to be wrong. I was still adjusting.

Each evening after work I would walk through the serene, staid streets of Zurich, which offered me space to muse and mull over all my new first premises.

Then the riots began. Suddenly my quiet, contemplative streets were filled with hundreds of young people who, night after night, battled police (I never did find out exactly what the fuss was all about). My first exposure began when I had inadvertently wandered around a corner where people were throwing rocks at the police. Because I was behind the police, the rocks that overshot them came toward me. I instantly took cover behind a statue, either of Ulrich Zwingli or of the Anabaptists (I don't remember which) whom he had killed for teaching adult immersion instead of infant baptism, a crime for which Zwingli had the offenders tied up, placed in boats, and drowned (whatever else you want to say about him,

17

the man truly had a sense of irony). Whomever the statue was of, it proved a good defense.

Despite the riots, I still took my evening walks. Though not exactly looking for the action, I didn't exactly avoid it either. With the exception of getting shot twice by rubber bullets, I came out pretty much unscathed.

There was, however, one close call. One night, when the rock-throwing and tear-gassing were about over, I walked past an alleyway where I saw three rioters—faces covered in masks—about to beat a man with pipes and clubs. Out of sheer desperation, I ran over and yelled, "Don't! Don't!" For my trouble one of the assailants threw me against the wall next to the impending victim. *Oh, man,* I thought, *isn't this just dandy.*

The one who first grabbed me then noticed something bulging under my coat. Perhaps thinking it was a weapon, he reached over and pulled it out. What he got was a large King James Bible (who else but a new believer would walk around with a humongous Bible under his coat, especially during a riot?). Seeing it, he started laughing hysterically. He then showed it to his two buddies, who, looking at the Bible, started laughing too. Reeking with hilarity, he handed me back the Bible. Lowering their clubs and pipes, all three turned around and walked away, splattering the darkness with shrill cackles and laughs.

With a dull, incomprehensible stare, the guy remaining looked at me and said, "Who are you? Where are you from?"

Still somewhat dazed myself, all I uttered was, "Hey, man, I just didn't want to see anyone get hurt, that's all." And then I just walked away (maybe I should have written that last sentence, "And then I left, riding tall in my saddle into the sunset").

For whatever reasons, I have rarely thought about the incident. Then earlier this year when I told it to Ulrich Frikart, president of the Euro-Africa Division (who is Swiss), he said, "Brother Goldstein—you should write this story up."

So I did (you just read it). The message? I'm not sure. Maybe it's about a lost opportunity. (Why didn't I witness to that guy?) Maybe it's about the power of the Word (it was, after all, the Bible that spared us from getting our heads bashed in). I don't know what to make of it all. I don't want to read more into than is there; nor do I want to dismiss it as nothing.

Suggestions, anyone?

The Swamp

After 18 years I recently returned to Gainesville, Florida, where I had first joined the Adventist Church.

Driving through town, I looked for the ramshackle room where one fiery dusk 20 years ago the Holy Spirit slipped past the walls and windows and with a gentle but tenacious love said that if I wanted God, if I wanted truth, then I had to burn the book that I had been furiously writing for more than two years.

I burned it, and though that smoke-filled room (nothing but a wooden box lifted off the ground by four concrete blocks) was where my life had taken a radical (six g's) gut-wrenching turn, I now had to drive around the block three times, until I realized that the place was gone, replaced by an apartment complex. It was as if the room, and I, had never been.

My dad called and said that he was selling his boat. Selling his boat? For my dad to sell his boat he must be getting old.

I drove a few blocks and parked the car, not having any change for the meter. I wandered over to the health food store where I had met the Adventists who brought me into the church. The store was no more; there was a bar/restaurant called The Swamp instead. I entered and stood in The Swamp, trying to reconstruct the place where I was first taught the gospel, where I first heard the three angels' messages, where I had wept as I read the prophecies that showed me the Bible was true, the place where even once (it had to be) an angel had come to comfort me. Looking (probably) like a loon about to pull out a gun and blow away the lunchtime crowd, I caught the attention of a waitress, who came over and asked if she could help. I said that this used to be a health food store where I had worked.

"Really?" she responded.

A few days before my return to Gainesville, I took my family skiing. My 10-year-old son and I skied down a slope with moguls like rough seas—and I couldn't keep up with him. How could this be? It seemed like just yesterday that I would pull this toddler's naked little half-Jewish tuckus out of the bathtub, stand him on the bathroom sink before the mirror, dry him off, and then, lifting his arms over his blond curly head, I'd shout, "You're a champ! You're a champ!" to which he'd shriek with hilarious glee. And now I'm eating this kid's snow?

Outside The Swamp, seeking something to let me know it wasn't a dream, that I really had once lived here, I walked up and down the sidewalk, looking for the graffiti that I had carved in wet concrete 23 years earlier. After wandering back and forth numerous times, I had to accept that it was gone, that I didn't even have indentations in dirty cement to show for my time here.

My dad called, said he was selling his house and moving into a condominium.

Looking up from the sidewalk, I felt like a phantom, as if I were only moody air, a sorry gust of nothingness, no more. It's then that the ultimate futility and meaninglessness of life, in and of itself, hit so clearly (it has been so long since I've been an atheist, I forgot what it's like). If this existence were all that there was, if our lives were capped, consummated, and climaxed by the grave, with no hope of anything beyond it—then all that happens before death is what Solomon called *hebel*, "vapor," or "breath," or "that which comes to nothing."

I wanted to find an old friend named Radical Bill, a half-homeless guy who had all but lived on the lawn of the University of Florida. Radical Bill was sort of an icon, a permanent fixture in the place. As I was walking, a homeless man hit me up for change. I gave him $2, then asked, "You know Radical Bill?"

"Heard of him," he answered.

"Have you seen him?" I asked.

"Nope," he said, shaking his head. "Haven't even heard him in years."

I returned to the car, pulled a parking ticket off the window, and left.

My dad called, said he has leukemia.

―∽―

Sheer Quantity of Trifle

When planning marriage, my future spouse and I decided that, for many reasons, we would live in her place, not mine. Before moving in, however, I said that the large square box filled with inane noise and light in the middle of the living room would have to go. I was referring, of course, to the television. She agreed.

That was about 16 years ago, and we've never been sorry. We lived without a TV before we had kids; we live without one now; and, if time should last, we'll be without one long after the kids are gone. Though I've made plenty of dumb choices in my life (how many people, for example, can turn a $2,700 stock investment into $45 in just six fun-filled weeks?), this decision to not own a television was one of the better ones, for sure.

Even before becoming an Adventist I rarely watched TV; mostly because I didn't have the time, and also because what I saw so strained credulity that I could barely believe that grown-ups had consciously collaborated to put this nonsense together. Even then, long before having any biblical impetus to guard the avenues of the soul, I decided that I didn't need the intellectual lobotomy that the boob tube offered.

Though time remains a factor, because it's hard enough for me, in even the best of environments, to keep my mind focused on heavenly things, a few hours a week of TV would be, I know, spiritually disastrous. My sanctification seems marginal enough at best now, even without a TV; I shudder to think what would happen if I had one.

I'm not judging people who do own and watch TVs. Many are a lot better followers of Christ than I am. I'm just not someone who can saturate their mind with hours of filth, violence, and profanity day after day and keep a semblance of a meaningful relationship with the Lord. I know, because the few times a year that I do watch television (usually when holed up in a hotel on a trip), I sense what it does to me spiritually, and it's about the *last* thing I need.

There are, for sure, some good things on TV (and Hitler built the Autobahn, too); I just don't need the added temptation of trying to find them amid the mindless, immoral inanity in which they are immersed.

A few years ago my dad—who, I guess, couldn't stand the thoughts of his grandchildren not having a TV—sent me one, with a built-in video player. I immediately removed the rabbit ears, virtually denuding it of TV qualities. We now have only a video player for the kids, and it's strictly policed.

Some well-meaning soul is probably asking, *What does this poor family do night after night without a TV?*

It's easy: we read books.

Sure, I admit that there are times I come home from work so tired I'd love to do nothing but sit in a chair and watch the mindless dribble that emanates from the television, but because I don't have that option, I usually just go to bed instead.

In Goethe's *Faust* a director, a poet, and a comic argue over the best way to produce a play. The director contends that they need to make the play popular, to get the largest number of people to watch, and the way to do that is, he says, to overwhelm them by "sheer quantity of trifle." In other words, give them as much stupidity as possible. Sounds like Hollywood's agenda, prime-time, and I refuse to be sucked into it.

As someone certainly not in a position to judge anyone about any-thing, I nevertheless throw out a challenge to my brothers and sisters: turn the TV off, even for a three-month trial (the advice I really want to give is more draconian, requiring a shotgun). See what happens. See how much more time you have for other, more fulfilling things (if nothing else, you will be able to read more). See how much more time you'll have for fam-ily or friends. See how much more the quality of your life improves. And see what happens to your relationship with God; it can only get better.

Trust me, at least on this one (for investment advice, however, defi-nitely go elsewhere).

—❧—

City Lights

Walking with my wife and offspring in San Francisco, I eyed a storefront sign that locked my knees stiff.

"City Lights Bookstore!" I howled. Having grown up in the sixties and seventies, filled with a mad desire to write fiction, burning with an obsessive love for poetry, and ignited by a feverous wanderlust that took me around the world by the tender age of 20, I felt like a medieval crusader in Jerusalem who thought he'd just found the spear that lanced Christ's side.

Opened in the early 1950s, City Lights became the center of the beat generation (from which the word "beatnik" was begotten), often consid-ered the forerunner to the hippie movement. Jack Kerouac, Allen Ginsberg, Neal Cassady, and William S. Burroughs, these were the avatars of beat, a fractious explosion of hedonistic defiance against a world that seemed de-void of meaning to men who longed to find some, even if, in the end, they looked for it in all the wrong places.

The uncontested Bible of the beats was Jack Kerouac's *On the Road* (1957). Recounting the years when he, Kerouac, took a series of cross-country trips, *On the Road* is a spasm of frenzied secular spirituality in which these characters, however awed at life, struggle to make sense of it.

"I had traveled 8,000 miles around the American continent," wrote

Kerouac, "and I was back in Times Square and right in the middle of rush hour, too, seeing with my innocent road eyes the absolute madness and fantastic hoorair of New York with millions and millions hustling forever for a buck among themselves, the mad dream—grabbing, taking, giving, sighing, dying, just so they could be buried in those awful cemetery cities beyond Long Island City."

It was atheist apologist Anthony Flew who argued that even if there was no meaning to life, there was meaning *in* it. Though human existence was, as a whole, purposeless, one could derive purpose out of each moment itself, even if nothing existed beyond the moment itself. *On the Road* is essentially about people who, knowing no purpose to life, sought it only in itself, in one another, and in the moments they experienced.

"The only people," wrote Kerouac, "for me are the mad ones, the ones who are mad to live, mad to talk, mad to be saved, desirous of everything at the same time, the ones who never yawn or say a commonplace thing but burn, burn, burn like fabulous yellow Roman candles exploding like spiders across the stars and you see the blue centerlight pop and everybody goes 'Awww!'"

Of course, a "spirituality" (Kerouac always insisted that the beats were "spiritual") that existed just "for the moment" must inevitably self-destruct into hedonism, exactly what happened to the beats. However much *On the Road* glamorized the partying, spontaneity, and sensuality, these things eventually destroyed them (and sometimes those they loved). Kerouac died from abdominal hemorrhaging brought on by alcoholism; age, 47. Neal Cassady, after a rainy night of drunken partying in Mexico, fell asleep on a railroad track and died in a hospital the next day; age, 42. William Burroughs, bragging about his marksmanship, put a glass on his wife's head and did a William Tell act that killed her with a single shot.

That leaves Allen Ginsberg, the only beat I ever saw in person. I heard Ginsberg read his poetry in the Milky Way Bar in Amsterdam a few months before my conversion. However beautiful his lyrics (one poem about burying his New York Jewish father, I, the son of a New York Jewish father, still vividly remember), Ginsberg spent half the time talking about homosexuality.

"He sounded," I said to a friend as we stepped into the Amsterdam night, "like a tired old man."

With this background, and with my wife and kids in tow, I entered City Lights. The place seemed dark, cavernous, sour, as if haunted by its sordid past. After a few minutes, having bought nothing, we left, and in the liberating California sunlight I felt so thankful that in my own quest for meaning, I found a road radically different from the one that led the beats to such a dead end.

~

Principles of Marriage

I t's easy for those who, like me, wander the earth preaching to appear so devout, so religious and pious from the pulpit. All it takes is a few right phrases, a few timely genuflections, a few holy quotes . . . and voilà! One can appear ready to float off to heaven.

What's not so easy, however, is to be so holy at home. Time and again I've had to tell myself, *If I can't be Christian at the house, particularly with my wife, then all the pious phrases, genuflections, and quotes from the pulpit mean nothing.*

The following are a few principles derived (homiletically, not exegetically) from Scripture about being Christian with our spouses—where (unlike the pulpit or any other public forum) it really counts.

1. "In whom we have redemption through his blood, the forgiveness of sins, according to the riches of his grace" (Eph. 1:7). One of the most crucial elements in any marriage is forgiveness. You must learn to forgive, especially when your spouse *doesn't* deserve it. Anyone can forgive the deserving; in fact, that's hardly forgiveness. True forgiveness is forgiving those who don't warrant it—the way the Lord forgives us through Christ. We must do likewise. Otherwise, our marriage, if it survives (which isn't likely), will seem like purgatory.

2. The second principle is related to the first. "For all have sinned, and come short of the glory of God" (Rom. 3:23). You must accept, out of the gate, that you're married to a sinner—to a being damaged to some degree emotionally, physically, and spiritually. Get used to it. Accept your spouse's faults. Pray your way through them. You might have to live with those faults, but you don't have to obsess over them. If you do, they will eat you alive. A holy and perfect God, through Christ, accepts us as we are; you, who are hardly holy and perfect, must do the same with your spouse.

3. "Look not every man on his own things, but every man also on the things of others. Let this mind be in you, which was also in Christ Jesus: who,

being in the form of God, thought it not robbery to be equal with God: but made himself of no reputation, and took upon him the form of a servant, and was made in the likeness of men: and being found in fashion as a man, he humbled himself, and became obedient unto death, even the death of the cross" (Phil. 2:4-8). The point is simple: don't always think of yourself first. Try to put your spouse before yourself, just as Christ put us before Himself. As sinful creatures, whenever a situation arises, our natural instinct is to think: *Oh, how will this affect me, me, me?* It's as natural as seeking water when thirsty. But through the grace of God you can learn to put your spouse and his or her needs before your own; this principle can greatly help any marriage.

4. The last principle is tied to the third: "For we have not an high priest which cannot be touched with the feeling of our infirmities; but was in all points tempted like as we are, yet without sin" (Heb. 4:15). Just as Christ put Himself in our situation, to best relate to us, we should do the same with our marriage partner. Try to view any given situation or crisis not just from your *own perspective* but from your spouse's. See how he or she views the situation, how it has an impact on him or her, and why he or she would feel about it the way he or she does. This principle can go a long way in alleviating tough situations.

Every marriage carries its own set of challenges, and no formula guarantees success. And, of course, I don't always perfectly apply these concepts in my own marriage (as my wife will readily attest). But by the often painful surrender of self through the vehicle of prayer, I do try. And by the grace of God, I find again and again that they do work.

Anyone can be Christian in public; only a true one can be one at home.

—∾—

Among the Loaves

As the old man's eyes (two raw sores upon which his forehead squatted) were touched by the genteel light from the loaves of factory-baked bread in factory bags sealed in factory ties—tears formed. Either like water they diluted his pain, or like glass they magnified it. I wasn't sure which.

"Praise the Lord!" he uttered, his curved fingers caressing the plastic. "Praise the Lord! I wanted bread this morning but had none, so I had to use pancake batter instead. And now, all of this! Oh, thank you."

Here we are, almost four centuries since the Puritans stole their first plot of land from the Native Americans in order to build their "city set on a hill," and now, in this American city, *an old man has to eat pancake batter because he doesn't have bread?*

Once, twice a month at most (just enough, I suppose, to assuage my conscience), my family and I ride into Baltimore to help Charles Henson, who has been feeding the city's hungry for more than 10 years now.

The poor, they are different from you and me. You can just see it in the way they walk, in the clumsy way they carry their fat, in the way they strain to smile. They live, it seems, closer to the center of the earth, and so gravity weighs heavier on them than on the rest of us.

A foreboding, a harshness, emanates from their streets, as if life took hold here against all odds. When we unload the bread, the pastry, the rolls, the poor dribble out from their abodes, unapologetic, unashamed, but polite and always thankful. They prefer white over whole-wheat, bread over rolls. Sweets are popular, especially among kids and junkies. When things get rowdy, as they sometimes do, it's never over the bread or rolls, but always over the cakes and cookies.

Recently a man, perhaps 30, hovered among the loaves. Pale, cold, he looked as if all his blood had drained out a hole and something unnatural, something synthetic, kept him upright. As I filled a bag with bread and handed it to him, I asked if he were OK.

"No," he said with a soft resignation, as if he had already bitterly resolved things. "I have AIDS. The doctors tell me that I'll be dead in a month. If I don't see you again in this life, I'll see you in the next."

A young man, 19, so cross-eyed I can still get a headache thinking about his gaze, stuffed a few pliant loaves in the bottom of a baby carriage. I asked about the mother; she was gone. The baby just had an operation on her stomach (I don't remember for what). The kid hated these streets, where he lived: "I get tired of the drug deals, and the shootings." He worked at a convenience store (one of the few among the loaves, it seemed, who was employed). He pointed down the street, toward the Ravens' football stadium, which rose like the Colosseum. He applied there for a job washing stands. "Maybe," he said, "I can one day be a supervisor of those who wash the stands."

And this was just one corner among miles of asphalt poverty, just one city among hundreds in the United States, the greatest economic power in history. Across borders billions *(billions)* would envy the affluence of him whose great hope was to one day supervise the washing of the stadium stands.

And this is only poverty. What about prisoners, refugees, suicides; what about the insane, the famished, the lonely; what about the dying, the diseased, and the depressed? "For where else," wrote Arthur Schopenhauer, "did Dante get the material for hell, if not from our real world?" Or, as Edna St. Vincent Millay wrote:

> "Anne, eat your breakfast;
> Dan, take your medicine;
> Life must go on;
> I forget just why."

There, among the loaves, and especially in that old man's eyes and in the young man's hopes, I saw more than ever why, when Christ returns, it isn't to repaint, refurbish, or reupholster, but to start all over . . . and nothing will remain of sin but the scars on His hands.

Twenty Years . . . and Counting

In 1980, after a passionate search for truth, I became a Seventh-day Adventist, a radical paradigm shift for an agnostic Jew who hated Christians—and vegetarians.

Three years later, when the North American Division needed someone who was Jewish, an Adventist, and a writer (they didn't have much to choose from, did they?), they approached me in their search for an editor of *The Israelite*. First begun in the 1950s as an outreach to Jews, *The Israelite* (now *Shabbat Shalom*) had long needed an overhaul (among its article titles were such classics as "What Does a Man Do While Dead?" or, my all-time favorite, "Is the Grand Canyon Really Old?").

After working on the magazine for a year, I was moved to the General Conference headquarters. It was 1984; I was 28. Within a few weeks, after someone canceled at the last minute (how I still get most of my speaking appointments) I was asked to do worship. Afterward, one of the secretaries, Ann Troy, said to me quietly, "Cliff, you're a fine speaker, but don't ever sing in public again." I took her at her word, and I never sing anywhere, ever, in public or private.

Not long afterward another secretary, Pat Orange, called me. At the time I would sit at my desk with my feet outside the open window. Someone complained because my shoes had holes in them, which wouldn't have been so bad except my socks did too, and I was asked to please take everything, dirty feet and all, down.

My worst experience came at Annual Council that first year. One of the guys who led me into the church called; he wanted to stay with me. He arrived, with a couple of people whom I didn't know. The next day, huge boxes, filled with dissident tracts, arrived at my door. Before I knew it, these people—picket signs in one hand, tracts in the other—traipsed out of my apartment and went straight to the General Conference building, where they stood outside picketing and haranguing delegates. One guy actually shouted Ellen White quotes at them. Done for the day, they would load up in their cars—and come back to my place.

Almost catatonic with angst, I pleaded, "Lord, please, please, if You don't let anyone know about this, I'll never eat chocolate, or cheese, again." The Lord kept up His end of the deal better than I did mine, and the council ended with my secret intact. My big fear, though, was, "Oh, no, suppose they want to come next year?" Fortunately, I soon got married, and the problem was solved, because my wife had little tolerance for what she deemed "all your weird friends."

Things quieted down (amazing what a woman will do for you) and besides editing *Shabbat Shalom,* I worked under *Liberty* editor Roland Hegstad. It was an extraordinary privilege, having him for 10 years pick apart everything I wrote. I must have learned something, though, because when he retired, they made me *Liberty* editor. Thus began six years of constant haranguing, in which I was accused of being everything from a Jesuit to a Communist and—worst of all—a Republican! I then decided I needed something less controversial, something everyone perfectly agreed upon, something in which I would face no more criticism, and what else could that be but to edit the Sabbath school quarterly (i.e., the *Adult Sabbath School Bible Study Guide*). After about half the theologians and editors in the church turned down the job (did they know something I didn't?), they gave it to me—and here I am six years later, accused of, well, you name it, I've been accused of it.

Outside of the constant sniping, the endless complaints, the rude phone calls, the nasty e-mails, and the thanklessness of the job itself—I love it. Why? I don't know; maybe it's subconscious penance on my part.

Anyway, 20 years at the General Conference, and I haven't been thrown out—yet. Talk about grace.

As I look back over these two decades, my biggest regret is the contrast between what I—in the Lord—could have become and what I still am. The Lord, I must assume, isn't done with me yet.

Thank God, eh?

Infinity's Twin

BOTH JEWISH TRADITION and Ellen White teach that Moses wrote the book of Job, even before Genesis. That makes sense, really, because for most people the question of pain and evil is more pressing than the question of cosmogony. Thus, after getting past the mess that is me, *The Mules That Angels Ride* delves into "theodicy," a fancy theological term for the justification of God in the face of evil and suffering. If God is omnipotent, omniscient, and all-loving, why is there evil? No doubt we who love God and believe in His goodness have struggled to work through this issue. These columns attempt to do just that. They are digitalized musings, thoughts, and ideas that have helped me, at least for now, understand the goodness and love of God despite evil and suffering. What more can I pray for other than that something in these pages will strike a chord in the heart of someone struggling with the same things, and that the fruit of my printed wrestling will help anyone who's seeking answers to what's, perhaps, the hardest of all faith questions.

Responses,
Retorts, Rebuttals

The common argument against the existence of God is *If God is all-loving and all-powerful, why is there evil?*

The common retort to that argument is: *God's love demands that He give His creatures freedom to choose.* It was in response to this retort that atheist apologist J. L. Mackie presented a fascinating rebuttal:

"If God has made men such," Mackie wrote, "that in their free choices they sometimes prefer what is good and sometimes what is evil, why could he have not made men such that they always freely choose the good? If there is no logical impossibility in a man's freely choosing the good on one, or on several occasions, there cannot be a logical impossibility in his freely choosing the good on every occasion. God was not, then, faced with a choice between making innocent automata and making beings who, in acting freely, would sometimes go wrong; there was open to him the obviously better position of making beings who would act freely but always go right. Clearly, his failure to avail himself of this possibility is inconsistent with his being both omnipotent and wholly good."

WOW! At first glance that sounds powerful. A second glance, however, reveals just how weak it is. Sure, God could have created beings who would choose only the good, but would they really be "free," and would what they choose really be "good"?

A person free to make only good choices is "free," but in the limited sense that a prisoner—if allowed to walk around their cell, use the toilet, or think whatever thoughts they want—is "free." A person locked in a dungeon is, in one sense, "free," in that their mind isn't chained to a wall. Jean-

31

The Mules That Angels Ride

Paul Sartre argued that even a person even under torture is "free" in whether or not to divulge information. Mackie's people are "free" in the way a poor person is "free" (along with a rich one) to sleep on a park bench. If one has a very narrow, parochial, and limited view of what it means to be free, Mackie has a good point. In contrast, a broader, deeper, and more-dimensional freedom saps Mackie's argument of vitality because people free to make only moral choices are not only not free but not even "good."

Can a person capable of only moral (or good) acts be moral (or good)? Or can coerced acts ever be moral? Did a person forced at gunpoint to give blood in order to save a life commit a moral act or just one that resulted in the good (in the same way that a tree blown over a bridge resulted in the good because it prevented a family from being killed in a wreck on the other side)? A computer can be programmed to do the good (such as warn of an air attack that gives innocent people time to find shelter), but is its action moral? Mackie's people, who can do only the good, who have no other choice than the good, are no different than actors who perform the "good" on stage. There's a thinness to their deeds that denudes them of virtue or "goodness."

If God wanted to create moral beings, free beings, good beings, He had to create them with a freedom much broader than Mackie's argument allows. Morality, to be morality, must possess the potential for immorality, just as goodness, to be good, must possess the potential to be not good. God could have created "men such that they always freely choose the good," but only in a universe in which the notions of "freely," "choose," and "the good" were cardboard cutouts of the real (and bad ones at that).

The core of Mackie's rebuttal is this: *No free person ever created by an omniscient and loving God should ever do immoral acts.* The core of my retort is this: Nothing in the notion of an all-loving and omnipotent God demands that the free beings created by Him must always do right. On the contrary, a loving and omnipotent God who creates moral and free beings has to, of necessity, place them in an environment in which evil, though not inevitable, must be possible. The definition of "moral" and "free" demands it. Otherwise, all God could have created were Mackie's gutless and amoral stick-figures who, in the end, are neither good nor free.

Perfection

Painfully etched on the front page of the Washington *Post* was a 12-year-old Bosnian boy who, having climbed down from a cherry tree, had stepped on a land mine that blew off two limbs.

But what caught my attention was—the cherry tree. Why? Because when I had become a believer, when the veil that had kept me lost in darkness all my life had first been lifted and I could suddenly see in nature irrefutable proof of a loving Creator, I was standing in a field in Denmark where, rising out of the earth, a cherry tree dangled luscious red cherries that glistened richly in the sun—and God's love couldn't have been more obvious to me than if an angel of light had plucked a piece of fruit from the branches and glided over to ease it between my lips.

So how could a child climb down from a cherry tree and have his limbs blown off? Or in more universal terms, why does evil exist in a world created by a good and perfect God?

Though the book of Job teaches that on this side of heaven, evil—especially in its particulars—appears random and meaningless, the book of Ezekiel explains how evil could arise in a universe originally created by a perfect God: "Thou wast *perfect* in thy ways," the Lord said to Lucifer, "from the day that thou wast created, till *iniquity* was found in thee" (Eze. 28:15).

But if Lucifer was created "perfect" (a perfect God is, after all, going to make only a perfect creation), how could iniquity be found in him? The answer is that the concept of "perfection" itself must include the *potential* for imperfection. In other words, perfection encompasses in its definition the potential for evil, for imperfection; otherwise, these never could have arisen. If perfection excluded the possibility of evil, evil would never be; the fact that evil exists proves its potentiality, even in a universe created perfect.

God, of course, didn't create sin; He created freedom, and freedom allowed the option to sin, which humans have chosen. Look at the Fall. Adam and Eve were molded in the perfect moral image of God. "In the image of God created he him; male and female created he them" (Gen. 1:27). The only way they could have fallen, then, was if the phrase "the image of God" (whatever that means) included within its meaning the possibility of sin, which it obviously did.

Ellen White wrote about inhabitants on another planet who were "noble, majestic, and lovely," and who "bore the express image of Jesus"

(*Early Writings,* pp. 39, 40). She also said that in their midst grew two trees, and that though these inhabitants "had power to eat of both," they were forbidden to eat from one. Thus included in nobility and majesty of perfect beings bearing the "express image of Jesus" was the potential for disobedience. They had the freedom, and the power, to disobey; if they didn't have that option, they wouldn't be perfect.

Jesus Himself personifies this point. Though literally the embodiment of perfection and sinlessness, didn't that perfection include the potential for imperfection, even sin? What purpose were His temptations ("He was in all points tempted like as we are" [Heb. 4:5]) if Christ couldn't have fallen? What type of example would Jesus be for us in our struggles with sin if He could not have sinned? The fact that Christ could have sinned proves that in God's moral universe perfection includes the possibility of imperfection.

Why? Because the foundation of God's government is love, and love—by its very definition—can't be forced, or else it's not love. The moment it's coerced it's no longer love. Thus if love is the motivating force behind God's perfect creation, then fundamental to the moral components of that creation is free will, and free will is not free if it doesn't include the potential for disobedience.

Love, of course, doesn't necessitate evil, only an environment—such as a perfect universe—that allows it, which goes a long way in explaining how a child can get his or her limbs blown off, even under the shadow of a cherry tree.

⁓

The
Rough Edges

Why does God allow us, mere packets of flesh and bone, blood and spirit, to be ravaged by the evil that sears flesh, crushes bones, embitters the blood, and exiles the spirit to wastelands of despair?

Who among even the most "remnant" of us hasn't wrestled with such a question? Each of us (if honest) would admit that it can, even if for only a few raw naked moments, bend our faith almost to the breaking point.

Even though we can jam ceaseless and macabre vignettes of death, pain, and mindless desolation into the overarching template of the great

34

controversy between good and evil, the edges still appear rough enough. Clouds of darkness to slip by and infest our tattered souls like some sort of metaphysical parasite of doubt.

The following words, slammed with ink into the page in your hands, attempt, however feebly, to help smooth those edges.

In his suicidal novel *Reader's Block,* David Markson (who also happens to be my uncle) quoted Nietzsche: "In the end one experiences only one's self."

Nietzsche's right. When we grieve with the grieving, sorrow with the sorrowing, and suffer with the suffering, it's still only our own grief, our own sorrow, and our own suffering we experience, never anyone else's. The "compassionate" catchphrase of the nineties, "I feel your pain," is a lie. We feel no one's pain but our own, even if that pain is over someone else's pain.

"What were you doing," asked Anne Dillard in *Harper's,* "on April 30, 1991, when a series of waves drowned 138,000 people? Where were you when you first heard the astounding, heartbreaking news? Who told you? What, seriatim, were your sensations? Who did you tell? Did you weep? Did your anguish last days or weeks?"

If you wept or anguished, it was still your own tears and anguish, not the tears and anguish of even a single one of those 138,000 victims; and not one of the 138,000 experienced a spark of the pain from any of the other 137,999 individuals. Whether starving alone on a deserted island, wasting away with leprosy, or gagging to death with dozens of others in a Nazi gas chamber—it's all the same. One experiences only oneself.

It's a Christian maxim that whatever we suffer now—divorce, death, job loss, health problems—God suffers *with us.* A fine thought, no doubt, and true; God is not indifferent to our fate. On the contrary.

But how does the Creator of the universe, on His throne in all His un-surpassed majesty, might, and glory—guiding the stars in their appointed paths, surrounded by "thousands and thousands times ten thousand times ten thousand" worshipful angels—relate to, for instance, the tormented and shattered world of a child as mommy and daddy divorce? How can the One sustaining Orion or spinning the Milky Way know the anguish of colon cancer?

Then there's Jesus: God as flesh, blood, bone, and spirit on the cross, dying a death, suffering a fate, and feeling an anguish so much worse, so much more intense, so much deeper, than anything any other individual— knowing only his or her own personal anguish—ever has or could. Jesus died the "second death," a trauma so much worse than anything the bitterness of life and the first death could ever bring to an individual's existence, no matter how wretched.

Jesus never had colon cancer. He never watched His parents divorce. He was never swept away on a "series of waves." These and endless others' woes were experienced by individuals who suffered only as much as individuals can. And nothing anyone has suffered individually was worse than what Christ, the Lord Himself, suffered as a human being punished for all the sins that produced these woes to begin with.

God Himself, embodied in our flesh, wired with our nerves, went through more pain, anguish, and despair than any of us individually ever could—a truth that may not answer all the questions about pain, but can at least help smooth some of the rough edges.

⌐∾⌐

The Angst of
the Unanswerable

April," wrote T. S. Eliot, "is the cruelest month." September, July, January (all the others, actually) are wretched too. Cruelty's not diurnal, nor suffering cyclical, like the moon's skull. Grief knows no lull, and maybe it's the accumulated haze of our cries (and not hydrocarbons) that causes the stars to flicker at night. The more people, the more pain: the correlation's impeccable.

For atheists and secularists, pain is just part of the progression, the inevitable side effects of an evolving species (like fumes to the internal combustion engine). No doubt secularists and atheists are appalled by pain, death, and loss, as is the Christian; they just have no problem explaining them.

In contrast, it's the Christian—with his or her all-powerful, all-knowing, and all-loving God—who cringes to fit even one child dying of AIDS, or of cancer, or of fire into the gentle palm of a loving heavenly Father, only to see that child crushed by titanic fingers.

I can't answer these questions, at least not with any more precision than what the great controversy motif—broad, universal, and all-encompassing—allows, but here's a thought that helps me to live, at least for now, with the angst of the unanswerable:

As humans, we experience only our own pain, only our own suffering, never anyone else's. No matter how closely tied to others, we can never splice into their nerves in order to feel a prick of their pain or a spasm of their woe. Whatever we feel for others, we feel it only in ourselves, only as ourselves. Other people's pain comes to us only, and always, as our own.

When thousands of people starved to death in an African famine, each individual mother, each individual father, each individual child, suffered only as an individual can suffer, feeling no more pain than an individual can feel. Though we are appalled at the staggering numbers of the worst human tragedies, in the end, no one among all these numbers to the left of the decimal point has ever suffered as anything other than a single digit. Whether crushing out the life of two people or 2 million, pain remains finite, hedged in always by what's as minuscule and as evanescent as the human. We know no more suffering than our personal metabolism allows, no more pain than our delirious cells can carry; the moment the threshold gets crossed, death cracks it off.

Only one exception exists to this otherwise pandemic personalization of pain—and that's Jesus on the cross, God in humanity carrying in Himself the pain and suffering of humanity. At Calvary the miseries of the entire world were, one by one, added up—and the gruesome sum fell on the Creator, God Himself, in the person of Jesus.

"Surely he hath borne our griefs, and carried our sorrows" (Isa. 53:4). That's all our griefs, that's all our sorrows, and they fell on the Lord Himself, who suffered more than any human being could ever suffer, because we can experience only our own pain, only our own suffering, while at the cross God experienced it all!

Here's the point: Human suffering comes from just one source, sin; and at the cross the sins of the world—and all the grief, wrath, and desolation inherent in those sins—honed in on Jesus, who as God endured the cumulative weight of them all. No matter how bad our suffering, or how many gigabytes of wide-eyed corpses on the evening news are crudely hewed in pixels across our consciousness, whatever we feel, either for ourselves or for others, we feel only as individuals. In contrast, God, on the cross, felt it all. At Calvary the Lord linked Himself to us through the essence of our humanity, that is, through our pain, only the level He experienced was greater and more intense than that which any other human being has ever known.

In the end, whatever moral freedom has cost humanity, it cost God more. And as I watch grief sculpt away without anesthesia the face of humanity (after all, it's the pain that does the hewing), the thought that the pain we know individually God knew corporately, though hardly resolving all the questions, helps me live with the angst of the unanswerable, even through the cruelest months.

⌁

Who Binds the Quarks

For morning devotion I've been praying, "Lord, talk to me through these texts" (Job 38-42).

We know what precedes them: the calamities, the pleas, the pain, the four foils even. When the Lord finally appears to Job (chapter 38), He says nothing about Satan's taunt, "Does Job fear God for no reason" (Job 1:9★) or about His own reply, "Behold, he is in your hand; only keep him alive" (Job 2:6). Instead, He unleashes a flow of rhetorical questions contrasting Him in His creative might and power to the transience and ignorance of poor Job.

"Where were you when I laid the foundations of the earth?" the Lord begins (Job 38:4). After echoing some of the earliest images in Genesis—i.e., the origins of the earth, the sea, light and darkness—He says to Job (basically), Of course you know all these things "because you were born then, and the number of yours days is great" (verse 21).

The Lord then points to wonders and mysteries of creation, again with a series of rhetorical questions ("From whose womb comes forth ice?" "Who has put wisdom in the inner parts?" "Who has put understanding in the mind?" "Does the eagle fly high at your command?")—not to prove His existence but only to show the vast gap between Job and the Creator. Had the book been written today, the Lord might have asked, "Who binds the quarks in protons and neutrons?" "Where were you when I first measured out a Planck mass?" "Is it by your wisdom that gravity bends space and time?"

When the divine litany's done, Job replies: "I know that You can do everything, and that no purpose of Yours can be thwarted. . . . I have heard of You by the hearing of the ear, but now my eyes have seen You; therefore, I despise myself, and repent in dust and ashes."

Thus, for Job, this vision of God was enough to convince him that the bemoaning about his dead children, his ruined property, and his diseased flesh was simply him bellyaching about "that which I did not understand, things too amazing for me that I didn't know."

Yet couldn't the God who makes the eagle fly, or who binds the quarks, have spared Job such suffering? Even with the great controversy motif unfolded in the background, the ending of Job still seems so inadequate, so full of unanswered questions. OK, God is great and powerful; we all know that. But if anything, that greatness and power make it even harder to understand human suffering.

For me, the only answer is the cross. For here we have the same God who revealed Himself to Job—the God who teaches the eagle to fly, the God who binds the quarks—suffering worse than any human being, even Job, ever suffered or could suffer. God does answer Satan's charges, not through the faithfulness of Job, but through the faithfulness of Jesus on the cross, where He bore our "griefs and carried our sorrows" (Isa. 53:4). The grief and sorrows that we know individually, He assumed corporately; thus, no one can lecture God on suffering, not when He in humanity bore in Himself the full brunt of all the suffering that sin has spread around the globe.

The God who asked Job, "Do you know the ordinances of heaven; can you establish their dominion on the earth?" becomes more incredible when we realize that through creating the "ordinances of heaven," He also took upon Himself earthly flesh and in that flesh died so that "he might destroy him who holds the power of death—that is, the devil" (Heb. 2:14, NIV).

Viewed through the cross, the book of Job makes more sense than without it, because the cross answers many questions that the book leaves unanswered. Job saw God as Creator; after the cross, we see Him as Creator and Redeemer, or particularly—the Creator who became our Redeemer (Phil. 2:6-8). Thus, like Job, only more so, what can we do before such a sight but exclaim: "I despise myself, and repent in dust and ashes"?

---

* The Hebrew translations in this column are those of the author.

Infinity's Twin

Talking to (or rather, writing about) a butterfly that quivered inside his clasp like a flame denuded of heat, Russian poet Joseph Brodsky mourned over the insect's brief existence:

> ". . . the date of
> your birth and when you faded
> in my cupped hand
> are one, not two dates.
> Thus calculated,
> your term is, simply stated,
> less than a day."

Yet, if the truth be known, Brodsky's lament wasn't over the butterfly, but over himself and over the nihilistic ratios that proportioned his life, the depressing computations that—no matter how artfully fudged or fervently prayed about—always added up to zero. "It's clear," he said to the butterfly, "that days for us are nothing, zeros." And zero added to zero 365 times, then multiplied by 60, 70, 90, or even 930 ("And all the days that Adam lived were nine hundred and thirty years" [Gen. 5:5]) still equals zero. And zero, as science writer Charles Seife called it, is "infinity's twin," and contrasted to infinity's twin, our days—or the butterfly's day—are nothing.

What Brodsky sensed, as the butterfly created "a frail and shifting buffer" between him and oblivion, was the similarity between his years and the butterfly's day when divided by eternity tilted. Over this divisor, his years, the butterfly's day, Adam's days of years (what's the difference?), all are swallowed up by one cold, unknown sum. If (as Galileo said) mathematics is the language of nature, then numbers become genocidal, and integers, dismal and damning.

If all human existence is divided by eternity—the lowest common denominator upon which all temporality rests, the continuum upon which all our moments, hours, days, years are plucked off like gray hair—then our lives must equal zero because anything temporal divided by the eternal comes to nothing.

The bottom line, the harshest fact, is that we are temporal entities in an eternal vat, and we flounder before our fate like beached fish. We're finite, and no matter how intently we twist, tweak, genuflect, and wail, we remain finite, and the finite divided by the infinite leaves nothing behind, nothing to the right (much less to the left) of the decimal point, no remainders to carry over (zero is the roundest of numbers). Poetic images of us, either as sparks, as dying leaves, as the "quintessence of dust," as vapors, attribute too much to us, at least in contrast to what the nihilistic number of eternity does to us, and that is, with one quick calculation, divide us into the nothing out of which we first came.

The earth is hungry. There's an essential equilibrium, a macabre ecological balance. Whatever we pull out of the earth, the earth pulls back out of us (gravity's the ground's best friend). Peel away the sky, pluck out the sun, the moon, and the stars, vacuum up the cold remnants of space and time—and what remains? Wealth, status, love, success, none are immune to the worms' rapacious burrowing. Dreams (miracles, too) don't escape the squirmy jaws. Even if our lives were bountiful, happy, fulfilled, an ascent from one triumph to another, from one joy to another, death still leaves it all in a well-trimmed dump . . . and the undertaker becomes a garbage man.

No wonder, then, that the New Testament comes laced with promises of eternal life (John 6:54; John 10:28; Luke 18:30; John 3:16; 1 John 5:13; 1 Tim. 1:16; Rom. 6:22; Titus 3:7, and on and on), for only the eternal guarantees restitution. A million years, even a billion years, might not possess enough good moments to make up for the bad suffered here. Eternity alone can balance all things out, and then some, because the infinite is more than the finite, and always infinitely so.

Paul wrote: "For our light affliction, which is but for a moment, worketh for us a far more exceeding and eternal weight of glory; while we look not at the things which are seen, but at the things which are not seen: for the things which are seen are temporal; but the things which are not seen are eternal" (2 Cor. 4:17, 18).

Our lives, the butterfly's life, these are fleeting, temporal; it's the unseen, the eternal, that can multiply this otherwise dismal sum into something greater than zero, even infinitely so.

hile we look not at the things which are seen, but at the things which are not seen: for the things which are seen are temporal; but the things which are not seen are eternal" (2 Cor. 4:17, 18).

Our lives, the butterfly's life, these are fleeting, temporal; it's the unseen, the eternal, that can multiply this otherwise dismal sum into something greater than zero, even infinitely so.

Klara Sara Goldstein

As a secular Jew I was raised on one religion alone: the Holocaust. The only burnt offerings I ever knew were those of Hebrew flesh; and incense? . . . It came in cans of Zyklon B. At age 12 I couldn't name the Ten Commandments; I could name every Nazi death camp.

Because I had been to Auschwitz thousands of times already (in the tormented imagination of a child defiled by history), when I finally did visit the place it was anticlimactic.

Except for one moment.

As part of the deception, the Nazis had told the Jews to write their names on their luggage in order to retrieve it on the other end. The other end, of course, was a smokestack.

There's a room at Auschwitz that exhibits some of the unclaimed baggage. As I entered, I stared at the floor and wondered, *Is there a Goldstein among the pile?* I lifted my head, and immediately my eyes fell on a trunk with the name Klara Sara Goldstein painted across it.

Klara Sara *Goldstein?*

Was Klara Sara a teenager, middle-aged, or elderly when killed? Married? Single? A mommy, perhaps? My distant relative? Had she been raped prior to being gassed and burned?

Maybe Klara Sara had accepted Jesus (for the Nazis, that didn't make a difference). She might have been, for all we know, an Adventist. More than likely, however, she probably never heard "the good news" at all.

I wonder, Was it chance or fate that placed her name, Klara Sara Goldstein, instead of mine, Clifford Ralph Goldstein on that baggage? Or my little daughter's, Hannah Emily Goldstein? Or my kid sister's, Shelly Louise Goldstein? Or my granddad's, Yitzak "Izzy" Goldstein?

For myself—whose belief in an omnipotent, omniscient God doesn't give much breathing space for things such as chance and fate—the question gets harder: Why, in the divine scheme, was I able to walk out of Auschwitz on my own free will (having already heard and accepted the gospel) while Klara Sara left, most likely, in a cloud of Christless smoke?

There is a word, coined by German philosopher Gottfried W. von Leibniz, called "theodicy," meaning "the justification of God." The idea behind it is that, when all is over, God will be proved just and fair in His dealings with Satan and rebellion. In other words, though evil has to be (at least for now, at least until its malignity is fully revealed), in the end God's love, mercy, and goodness, triumphing over evil, will be vindicated.

It's easy to wonder, of course, What's taking so long? How many more Klara Sara Goldsteins are needed to reveal the fruit of evil? *We get the point now!*

Yet the questions about God that need answers need these answers for, literally, eternity. All the universe, maybe even newly created beings, must be able to look back—no matter how far removed chronologically from the great controversy—and see the results of disobedience. Time tends to blur things; the more distant the past, the more fuzzy it appears. Evil has to unfurl itself so completely that billions of years after it's gone the heavenly intelligences in the farthest crannies will have no questions regarding it. Its demonstration needs to be so dramatic, so consummate and terminal, that God's love, mercy, and justice in dealing with it will satisfy all creation, over all the cosmos, for all eternity.

Until then the hard questions remain; it will take time to answer them fully, precisely because they *are* so hard. All we can do in the meantime is reach out by faith and trust God for those things that for now seem so incomplete.

Austrian mathematician Kurt Gödel showed that in mathematics some things cannot be proved true, even if known to be true. Gödel revealed a fundamental "incompleteness" that exists even in mathematics. Thus if something so basic as math leaves unanswered questions, why be surprised that something so much bigger and broader as God Himself would to the same, if not more so? The crucial difference, however, is that unlike math, which gives no promise of answers—God does.

And one answer I want will be about this unfortunate woman, Klara Sara *Goldstein,* and why her name was painted on that suitcase instead of mine.

The Openness of God

When Jesus said to Peter that "this very night, before the cock crows, you will deny me three times" (Matt. 26:34, RSV), did Peter have any choice other than to deny Jesus three times? If

Peter would have changed his mind, then so much for Jesus' omniscience; if he couldn't, so much for Peter's free will.

Questions about free will, fate, and God's foreknowledge have been pricking our neurons for millennia. All through Homer fate dogs the heroes of the *Iliad* and the *Odyssey*. Sophocles, in *Oedipus Rex,* wrote about a prophecy given to Laius and Jocasta that warned that their infant son Oedipus will grow up to kill his father and marry his mother. Despite everyone doing everything to prevent this tragedy, sure enough, by the play's end, Oedipus had killed his father and married his mother. Meanwhile, theologians through the centuries have grappled with the tension between freedom and the providences of an all-knowing, all-powerful God.

The problem reached a slow burn following the Newtonian revolution, in which immutable natural laws were believed to determine everything, including human actions (Voltaire thought it strange that all nature should obey eternal laws, while "a little animal, five feet high, . . . in contempt of these laws, could act as he pleased, solely according to his caprice"). This determinism was blindsided in the twentieth century by quantum physics, which showed that at the most fundamental levels reality exists as a statistic, a probability, nothing more—a concept that ignited new and even more disturbing questions about free will and fate.

Recently, in an attempt to alleviate tension between free will and God's foreknowledge, "open theists" have proposed that certain future events are not known by God because they don't yet exist. God knows, they argue, all of the future that's knowable; some aspects of the future, particularly those that deal with human free will and moral choices, are unknown to God because they have no existence. As Gregory Boyd expressed it: "The dispute is thus not over whether God knows everything, but rather over what constitutes the 'everything' which God perfectly knows."

Open theism is a well-meaning attempt to answer such difficult questions as Why does a God who knows everything "repent" or change His mind (Gen. 6:6; Ex. 32:14) depending upon circumstances? or How can we have free will if God knows our choices beforehand?

For what it's worth, as far as that last question is concerned I would argue that far from denying our free will, the Lord's perfect knowledge of our choices is what protects it.

Take Jesus and Peter. Could Peter have changed his mind and not denied Jesus three times? Of course he could have, but Jesus—knowing the future perfectly, knowing every neuron in Peter's brain, knowing of all the potential outcomes—told Peter what he was going to do because He knew beforehand what Peter was going to do. If Peter, using his free will, wasn't going to deny Him, then Jesus, knowing the future, wouldn't have said it.

On the other hand, suppose Jesus—not knowing Peter's choice because it didn't yet exist—told Peter that he was going to deny Him, but Peter, using his free will, started to move in another direction. Jesus would then have had to infringe upon Peter's free will in order to get him to do what Jesus said he would. Thus, at least in this case, God's absolute foreknowledge is what preserved free will.

Questions about the future are, really, questions about the nature of time: What is it? Does it have a beginning? an end? Relativity and quantum physics have radically revised our commonsense notions of time. Some physicists even argue that the past and the future are all illusions, and that time doesn't even exist at all.

Who know? And we mortals, "open" or classical theists, shouldn't be too dogmatic in our answers. Perhaps, in all our metaphysical musings, we should remember Milton's words:

"In thoughts more elevate, and reasoned high
Of providence, foreknowledge, free will, and fate,
Fixed fate, free will, foreknowledge absolute,
And found no end, in wandering mazes lost."

～

"Waxey" Gordon and the Mysteries of God

If you're reading this column, thank a Jewish mobster named "Waxey" Gordon.

The year was 1937. My dad, 12 years old, was hitchhiking in upstate New York with another kid. Two drunks picked them up and, as they sped along the winding, hilly roads of the Catskill Mountains the driver lost control and wrapped the car around a tree. The adults were unhurt; the two kids, in the back, were critically injured. My dad had, among other things, a broken back and a split skull.

Their precarious condition worsened when, at the hospital, the doctor refused to work on them until he knew who was going to pay. That, however, was the wrong attitude, because the other dying kid's brother was the notorious "Waxey" Gordon, a leader of the Jewish mafia. Though fading away after the war (because—unlike their Italian competitors, who usually brought their children into the family "business"—these Jewish gangsters sent theirs to college), the Jewish mafia in the heydays of the 1930s was brutal, making Al Capone's gangs look like nothing but wayward deacons pilfering change from collection plates. "Waxey," among the worst, came to the hospital, pulled the doctor aside, and said, "If either one of those kids dies, you're next." Ben Casey got the point, and both boys pulled through.

If, though, my dad had died, which he probably would have otherwise, I wouldn't be here. Thus, it seems that I, at least in part, owe my existence to a Jewish gangster from the 1930s. All of which raises a number of questions about the mysteries of God's providence.

Did the Lord—knowing the beginning from the end, knowing that decades later one of those injured kids would have a son who would accept Christ—use this thug to fulfill His will? Did He *need* the mobster to ensure my eventual existence, or could He have sustained my dad in another way? And if He could have (and I assume He could), then why did He (if He did) use such a scoundrel to fulfill His providence?

These, and innumerable other like questions, are "mysteries" of God's providences, things that we can't understand but that, if accepted by faith, will increase our awe of the power and wisdom of God. On the other hand, if taken with skepticism and incredulity, these mysteries will cripple us in doubt. The world is too big—too many forces have for too long been unleashed for us to unravel the strands well enough to be able to make sense of them. If we don't learn to trust God with the unknowns, they will converge into a confluence of empty, meaningless events that will suck out faith until only dead echoes of the Spirit remain within.

If there is no God, and we are just the random conclusions of all that preceded us, then there's no hope of answers more meaningful than lottery odds, because when you peel away the layers you find at the bottom only chance, cold statistics, nothing more. Without God, there are no mysteries, just things unknown, because the odds behind them are unknown and will probably remain so long after we die.

As Christians, though, we live not only with these mysteries but also with the promise that these mysteries will be unraveled, and that the answers unfolded from within them will quell every doubt and evaporate every fear. We are promised that God shall "bring to light the hidden

The Mules That Angels Ride

AS A TEENAGER I was always fascinated with the nature of belief, especially religious belief. How was it that many people, raised and educated in the same culture as I was, could believe in God and in the teachings of religion, something that was so alien, even repugnant, to me? In this section—as one of those who now believe in God and in the teachings of religion (ours)—I give the reasons for believing what I do. And, fascinatingly enough, one of the reasons is reason itself, or should I say "the shortcomings of reason itself." Over the years reason has led me to see the limits of reason in discerning truth. That is, it's only reasonable to see that reason can't answer everything. Whatever we believe—either secular or sacred—sooner or later we need to reach out in faith, because sooner or later we all come to givens, things we believe but can't prove. If these limits occur, for instance, even in math (which they do) how much more so in our religion, which takes us to realms more mysterious than $2 + 2 = 4$? These ideas, along with similar themes, are explored here. Again, despite some of the esoteric mumbo jumbo, I hope something in these pages will be what someone struggling with these questions just needed to read.

Where Angels
Fear to Tread

E very theory, philosophical or otherwise," wrote Stewart Shapiro, "must take some notions for granted" *(Philosophy of Mathematics)*. He's right. We all start with presuppositions, with things too fundamental to be provable; otherwise, what you proved it with would be your starting point, and on and on ad infinitum. You have to stop somewhere because you have to start somewhere.

For me, that starting point is the Scriptures. It was apart from the Scriptures that God first showed me He was real, that He was close, and that He cared. Immediately afterward, He brought me to the Bible, His most complete, explanatory, and convincing revelation to us, at least until we see Him "face to face" (1 Cor. 13:12). Until then Scripture's my starting point, the foundation through which everything about God needs to be filtered, interpreted, judged.

Of course, unanswered questions about the Bible remain. So what? Anything you know or believe, secular or religious, is dogged by unanswered questions. How much more so, then, the Word of God—which pulls back the curtain on unseen physical and spiritual realities? If seen realities, known principles that can be expressed as mathematical equations, come heavy-laden with baffling black holes that swallow all attempted explanations, how banal and hubristic to think that spiritual truths about unseen cosmic realities would be any different, especially for fallen beings who in their empiric brilliance (with a few Hellenistic exceptions) needed thousands of years to finally discern that the earth moved around the sun, not vice versa.

Scripture is, for me, the bottom line. I refuse to try to get under it, be-

49

hind it, and work at it from below, because whatever tools I use, they then become my first principles, the devices, the –isms, with which I judge Scripture. This is, basically, the historical critical project, and when I see where it has led, and the conclusions it has spawned, the quote from Alexander Pope, about fools rushing where angels fear to tread, does pirouettes through my head.

Everything from the divinity of Christ, the virgin birth, the Exodus, the covenant at Sinai, blood atonement, the resurrection, a six-day creation, predictive prophecy, you name it, and higher critics, using their man-made intellectual devices, have argued that it never happened or have spun it in a manner that denudes these truths of any salvific value. Nothing sacred is sacred; everything's up for grabs that doesn't fit with the latest method, the latest theory, that wipes out everything in its path until that theory is replaced by a new one, often based on different or even contradictory premises than the one just dumped into the intellectual trash heap. When all's said and done, what's left? Nothing.

Take the Jesus Seminar, which, using the latest and greatest critical tools, determined that Jesus wasn't resurrected but, instead, dogs ate His body. The sad thing is, people actually take these ideas, and others like them, seriously. Right now, for example, an Episcopal church in America is divided over whether Christ was really raised from the dead, or whether the Resurrection was just a myth, a symbol of some grandiloquent spiritual truth. Ideas, even bad ones, do have consequences.

Of course, reason, logic, history, experience, linguistics, science all have their roles; they just need to be judged and filtered by Scripture, not vice versa. Because all these things, to one degree or another, are just human concoctions whose authority rests only on the human sources that codify them. Or, as my uncle (David Markson) expressed it in his experimental novel, *Vanishing Point:* "Thomas Hardy's anecdote about looking up a word in the dictionary because he wasn't certain it existed—and finding that he himself was the only authority cited for its usage." Higher criticism works basically the same way. With higher criticism the method is the message. The higher critics tell us nothing about God, but a lot about ourselves.

I anticipate a barrage of attacks in response to this column from the usual suspects. One independent journal, for instance, recently lambasted me as a "fundamentalist" over my position on Creation.

Fine. But looking at the results of higher criticism, I'd rather be a "fundy" than a fool.

~

"Of Things Not Seen . . ."

The most important thing we can ever know, salvation in Christ, we know only by faith, a concept that, by definition, comes alloyed with uncertainty. It's a strange universe, ours, when the only knowledge that divides heaven from hell cannot be proved, at least not the way it can be proved that 70 cents is less than 80 cents. Correct change can be certain—but salvation is known only by faith? Why?

Given the nature of things, it's hard to see how it could be any other way.

For example, imagine if the words *Jesus Christ, the Son of God, died for the sins of the world!* . . . were written every day across the sky in every land, in every language, by a means that eluded rational, scientific explanation. What a powerful testimony, to be sure. Yet it would still require faith to believe that *Jesus Christ, the Son of God, died for the sins of the world,* would it not? Those miraculous letters wouldn't make the truth of His death absolute, any more than a voice shouting from the sky in every language, in every land, *Jesus Christ, the Son of God, died for the sins of the world* would either.

Suppose an angel, all tenderness and translucence, appeared before you and talked about Jesus' perfect sacrifice, then promised that Jesus would return soon. Would not that experience increase your faith? Your what? Faith? You'd need faith, even after that? Of course.

Scripture asserts that "faith is the substance of things hoped for, the evidence of things not seen" (Heb. 11:1). Our two great hopes, Christ's death on the cross and the Second Coming, are two things that we haven't seen. How can we believe them other than by faith? Even though those who witnessed Christ's death, His post-Resurrection appearances, and His ascension didn't need faith to believe in those events themselves—they needed it to believe that He was who He said He was, that His death had atoned for their sins, and that He would return in the clouds of heaven, as He promised. And if those who were at the cross needed faith, we—who weren't—surely do too.

What could possibly make our belief absolutely certain? Letters written and voices echoing from the sky? I don't think so. Angels in our faces? I don't think so. If, as Jesus said, the dead resurrected wouldn't cause some folk to believe, it's hard to see, considering the nature of our belief (about an event in the past that promises an event in the future), what could make this belief so certain that faith would be unnecessary.

Our deceitful hearts' biggest deceit is to downplay their own deceit-fulness. What we often call honest questions are mere cloaks for a polluted conscience. Lust, passion, pride—these are the witching chords that incite doubt within us. Disbelief is always easier than belief, especially in things that you have never seen, and especially when those same things whistle at our aberrant urges.

Whatever we've been given, or could ever be given, it would never be enough to make faith redundant. The witness of predicative prophecy, the testimony of nature, the evidence from history, our personal experiences of God's mercy and grace, even miracles are all part of a continuum, and no matter where we are on that continuum it's never, at least now, at absolute certainty. There's always room for more. It's like trying to go from the number 1 to the number 2 by halving each step; you'll never make it.

If, though, judgment, condemnation, and destruction are coming, there must be enough reason to have faith, because a just and fair God isn't going to punish anyone who doesn't deserve it. Hell, in a just universe, de-mands of the damned accountability; those who perish do so only because they rejected what could have spared them.

Someone once asked the twentieth century's most famous atheist, Bertrand Russell, what he would respond if, in the end, there was a God who said to him in the judgment, "Why didn't you believe in Me?"

"I would answer," Russell said, "'Because there just wasn't enough evidence.'"

Wrong.

The Mules
That Angels Ride

Poets can reach places inside me that I didn't even know existed until their verse unearthed and exposed them. Not all poets, of course (and certainly not all poems); but some poems by some poets slip past barriers and touch things inside me previously untouched because they were, previously, unknown.

One of the most penetrating of these intruders is Wallace Stevens, which is quite amazing because—unlike French gun-running bard

The Mules That Angels Ride

Rimbaud, or the hard-drinking and gambling Edgar Allan Poe—Wallace Stevens was, of all things, an insurance company executive. He's just not like any insurance company executive that I've ever read.

Yet Stevens was a rank evangelistic atheist. So many times, immersed amid his verse, I wanted to shout, "No! No! Wallace, you didn't understand Jesus!"

In, for instance, "Le Monocle de Mon Oncle" he wrote:

> "The mules that angels ride come slowly down
> The blazing passes, from beyond the sun.
> Descensions of their tinkling bells arrive.
> These muleteers are dainty of their way.
> Meantime, centurions guffaw and beat
> Their shrilling tankards on the table-boards.
> This parable, in sense, amounts to this:
> The honey of heaven may or may not come,
> But that of the earth both comes and goes at once."

No, Wallace! The parable amounts to this: Because of Jesus, because of what He accomplished at the cross, because of the promises that we have from Him now, the "honey of heaven" has already come. You just missed it.

In "The Worms at Heaven's Gate" Wallace wrote:

> "Out of the tomb, we bring Badroulbadour,
> Within our bellies, we her chariot.
> Here is an eye. And here are, one by one,
> The lashes of that eye and its white lid.
> Here is the cheek on which that lid declined,
> And, finger after finger, here, the hand,
> The genius of that cheek. Here are the lips,
> The bundle of the body and the feet.
>   ★ ★ ★
> Out of the tomb we bring Badroulbadour."

No, no, Wallace. Because of Jesus, that's not how we reach "heaven's gate," not even close. We'll arrive at that gate by the same glorious power that took Jesus there. Christ's ascension guarantees ours, in a body made new and incorruptible, not one that's transported in the entrails of worms.

The Mules That Angels Ride

You got it wrong, Wallace, wrong!
In "Sunday Morning" the poet wrote:

> "What is divinity if it can come
> Only in silent shadows and in dreams?"

No, no, no! Divinity came, not in silent shadows and in dreams, but in the flesh and blood of the Man Jesus Christ, God in the flesh, who lived among us to reveal Himself in all His unselfish, self-sacrificing love. You're looking for God, Wallace, in all the wrong places.
In "Negation" he outrageously wrote:

> "Hi! The creator too is blind,
> Struggling toward his harmonious whole,
> Rejecting intermediate parts,
> Horrors and falsities and wrongs;
> Incapable master of all force,
> Too vague idealist . . ."

Sorry, Wallace, but almost 2,000 years ago the Creator stepped into the "intermediate parts," where He at the cross experienced all the "horrors and falsities and wrongs" in ways none of us ever can imagine. You live by sight, Wallace, not by faith—that's why you haven't glimpsed divinity.
With his harboring such sentiments, it's no wonder that in "The Sad Strains of a Gay Waltz" he caught the dilemma of all those who refuse to see:

> "These voices crying without knowing for what,
> Except to be happy, without knowing how."

What they're crying for (without knowing it) are "the mules that angels ride" . . . and the happiness they want; it comes only in "the honey of heaven."

The Request

Having been hewed and chiseled (from womb to new birth) by the hard and graceless hammer of agnosticism, I found in the writings of Frenchman Albert Camus someone who could with eloquence and passion express the fear, the exasperation, and the pain that came from living in a world that—by its cruel and arbitrary nature—demanded many answers but didn't render any.

In a book recounting my own conversion experience I talked about Camus's influence on me during my college years: "Albert Camus is my Horus," I wrote, "chief deity in my expanding pantheon of philosophical polytheism. He asked all the right questions, expressed all the right fears. In Camus I see myself stomping the ground or shaking a fist at the sky, except that he does it so eloquently. But amid all his beautiful prose, I find no answers. He only better defines my anxieties. He opens up my wounds, shows me clearly my pain, but leaves me bleeding worse than before."

Killed in a car wreck in 1960 at the height of his fame and literary prowess (an absurd yet fitting death for someone whose basic theme was the absurdity of human existence), Camus had struggled to live a life that was, he believed, basically meaningless. He wrestled with what he called "this absurd, godless world," one that taunted us with intimations of meaning and purpose, and yet—spinning at more than 1,000 miles per hour—moved too fast for us to be able to grasp any. All we could rifle from the bowels of the earth, it seemed, were artifacts of our own emptiness and the cold trinkets of death.

No wonder, then, that Camus began one of his most famous essays with these two lines: "There is but one truly serious philosophical problem, and that is suicide. Judging whether life is or is not worth living amounts to answering the fundamental question of philosophy." However seemingly absurd, given his premises—which are that there is no God and that life has no purpose—one would be hard pressed to rebut this conclusion with any terminal logic.

In his novel *The Plague,* Camus, after describing a child's horrific death, created a scene in which a Jesuit (who symbolized Christianity) defended the incident. "That sort of thing is revolting," said Father Paneloux, "because it passes our understanding. But perhaps we should love what we cannot understand." Later in a sermon the priest said that though the suffering of the child was terrible, "since it was God's will, we too should will it."

After becoming a believer, I felt this burning frustration, this painful desire, to talk to Camus, to explain that this view of God, as expressed by Father Paneloux, was so wrong. How I wished I could have had three days with him, three intense days to tell him about the great controversy, about theodicy, about the freedom that love demands, and specifically about the cross and what happened there. Of course, Camus had already been dead 20 years, so I had to get over it.

Imagine, then, my astounded and jubilant amazement when I recently read about a Methodist minister who in a new book claims that Camus privately sought him out, had Bible studies with him—and had even requested a secret baptism. Albert Camus wanting baptism? It's like Yassir Arafat wanting a bar mitzvah.

And yet I'm not utterly surprised, because Camus's sincerity, his painful desire for answers, his zealous quest for truth, which all came through so forcefully in his writings, made him a prime candidate for the work of the Holy Spirit. Camus, however, died a few months after the request; thus, as far as we know, he never made it into a baptismal tank.

Nevertheless, what a wonderful testimony to the powerful, even if at times subtle, wooing of the Holy Spirit. When I first read about Camus's request, this verse flickered behind my eyes in cold black neon: "There was the true Light which, coming into the world, enlightens every man" (John 1:9, NASB).

That's *every* man, even the one who once wrote: "The silence of the universe has led me to conclude that the world is without meaning." Apparently, amid that silence he was beginning to hear something after all . . .

⊸⊷⊸

"What Is Truth?"

Standing in one of my favorite places (the philosophy section of the Briarwood used bookstore in Annapolis Maryland), I struck up a conversation with a psychologist. While discussing the theory of human evolution, he uttered these sounds: "Everything is a lie."

I mulled over this string of vowels and consonants for days, and decided that two problems existed with it (actually, there were three, but I've forgotten the third).

First, if everything is a lie, that must include the statement "Everything is a lie." Thus if "Everything is a lie" is a lie, then at least something must be true.

Second, how can a lie exist without truth existing as well? How could the sentence "The sun is cold" be a lie if, in fact, the sun were not cold? A lie can be a lie only if some existent truth makes it so. "All men are purple" is a lie, but only because a specific truth exists, in this case the truth being that some men are not purple. The notion of a "lie" means that what's being said isn't true, and the only way it can't be true is if some contrary fact existed. Thus the word "lie" itself, by its own meaning, denotes the existence of truth.

For Seventh-day Adventists, of course, it's no great revelation that truth exists (in fact, we even claim to *have* it). Yet the concept of "truth" itself is problematic. Various theories exist—the correspondence theory, the coherence theory, the pragmatic theory, and the deflationary theory—regarding what "truth" means. This debate isn't over what is true, but over what it means to say that something is "true."

Pilate's question "What is truth?" (John 18:38), directed at Him who said, "I am . . . the truth" (John 14:6), exemplifies two radically different notions of what "truth" means. Pilate expressed the typical Greek concept of truth as propositional (2 + 2 = 4, or "All bodies are extended," or "If a = b, and b = c, then a = c). In contrast, by referring to Himself as "the truth," Jesus taught that truth is a person—not an easy concept to grasp, especially for those reared in the Greek tradition, which viewed truth as propositions only.

What did Jesus mean when He said that He was "the truth"? How can "truth" be a person, even a person who is God? Who knows? But I see two possible approaches.

First, Scripture teaches that through Christ all things were created: "For by him were all things created, that are in heaven, and that are in earth, visible and invisible, whether they be thrones, or dominions, or principalities, or powers: all things were created by him, and for him" (Col. 1:16). All that exists, then, exists only in, by, and through Christ; nothing is real apart from Him. He alone has pure objectivity, pure knowledge, pure reality. In this sense, Jesus is the truth: truth exists only by virtue of the fact that He has created any and all things that can, indeed, be true.

Another approach, less metaphysical and propositional, comes from how the word "truth" *(emet)* is used in the Hebrew Scriptures. Repeatedly in Hebrew *emet* (truth) appears synonymous with the word *hesed,* or "lovingkindness."

"For thy lovingkindness *(hesed)* is before mine eyes: and I have walked in thy truth *(emet)*" (Ps. 26:3). "I have not concealed thy lovingkindness *(hesed)* and thy truth *(emet)* from the great congregation" (Ps. 40:10). "All the paths of the Lord are mercy *(hesed)* and truth *(emet)* unto such as keep his covenant and his testimonies" (Ps. 25:10).

In this context, truth isn't so much what we believe, or which propositions we hold, but what we are, what we do. Jesus was the perfect embodiment of *hesed;* His entire life, death, and high priestly ministry express *hesed.* Though propositional truth helps us understand *hesed,* if *hesed* and *emet* are so closely linked, then truth is something much more human, much more personal, much more relational than mere elucidation of doctrine. Who "had" the truth, the good Samaritan or the Levite? Who "has" the truth, a nasty Sabbathkeeper or a Sunday-worshipper demonstrating *hesed?*

No doubt, and contrary to my friend in the bookstore, truth exists, even eternal transcendent truth. The question we need to ask ourselves is—What does it mean to possess that truth?

God, Gödel, and Grace

Convinced that people were poisoning him, a strange little Austrian named Kurt Gödel starved himself to death, but not before publishing in 1931 "On Formally Undecidable Propositions on Principia Mathematica and Related Systems," which not only shook the foundation of Western thought but has made faith so much easier for me even though, beyond the first paragraph, I barely understand a word of what he wrote.

Let me back up.

Since Euclid (300 B.C. or so), mathematicians have used what's been dubbed the "axiomatic method," that is, starting with a few axioms or postulates, fundamental and self-evident truths, and then, proceeding with pure logic, they construct numerous correct propositions and theorems about any given system. For thousands of years this method worked so well with geometry that, eventually, it was applied all through mathematics.

Everything climaxed in the early 1900s, when Bertrand Russell and Alfred North Whitehead published their three-volume *Principia Mathematica,* which had (they believed) placed mathematics on a pure, logical foundation. After all, if math can't be grounded in logic, what can? With the *Principia,* humanity finally found a sure footing for truth, an immovable platform for certainty.

Not quite. Young Kurt Gödel, with his revolutionary paper, proved that within any given mathematical system, there will always be certain propositions or statements that can't be proved or disproved using the rules of that system. Sure, you might be able to prove all the propositions and axioms in your system by going *outside* to a new and larger system, but then that new and larger system will have its own statements that can be proved only by a new and larger system outside of that one, and on and on forever.

"In effect, then," wrote Douglas Hofstadter, "Gödel destroyed the hopes of those who believed that mathematical thinking is capturable by the rigidity of axiomatic systems, and he thereby forced mathematicians, logicians, and philosophers to explore the mysteriously new chasm irrevocably separating provability from truth."

What this means is that knowledge of even simple mathematics remains incomplete, and so one can never be certain that the axioms of arithmetic will not contradict each other. In other words, even in something as rigid and logical as math, some aspects just can't be "proved." How incredibly revelatory that even cold hard math—supposedly the foundation of all certainty (there's a reason some of the twentieth century's greatest philosophers were mathematicians)—comes with intrinsic, inescapable contingencies.

This Gödelian principle (called Gödel's Incompleteness Theorem) permeates reality. When, for instance, you put your garbage out, why doesn't the garbage collector take the can, too? Or how do you define a word other than with another word? But how do you define that other word but with another word, and on and on in a vicious, inescapable circle. Paul wrote about a Cretian who said that "the Cretians are always liars" (Titus 1:12). If the Cretian's statement is true, it has to be false, because Cretians, including the one whom Paul quoted, are *always* liars. Also, how can you prove something is true without pointing to a criterion that validates it? But how can you prove that whatever validates it is true without pointing to something that validates that new criterion, and on and on in infinite regress, or until we reach that which is inexplicable because it was before every explanation and had no origin or antecedent but was predicated on no cause because it was prior to all causes (and we all know who that is).

Almost every where I look, Gödel's shadow leaps from the grave. Many times in the margins of things I read I scribble, "Gödel!" He's been mentioned in many of my *Review* columns. I even just wrote a book called *God, Gödel, and Grace: A Philosophy of Faith*. What I have found so fascinating is that by revealing the inherent incompleteness in our ability to know anything, and by even mathematizing that incompleteness, Gödel showed that the need for faith—belief "in things not seen" (Heb. 11:1)—is fundamental to all human experience, not just religious ones. If incompleteness exists even in our understanding of numbers, why should I fret over the things I can't understand about the God who created those numbers?

I don't—and thanks to Gödel it's easier not to.

Waiting (Still) for Godot

The final week in my last class before I graduated from the University of Florida (1978), we studied Samuel Beckett's play *Waiting for Godot*. Literally days away from entering upon the real world (with nothing but a B.A. in English!), I was more concerned about eating than this two-act play, which is why I remembered nothing about it.

Two months later, sleeping in some bushes along a wall in Athens, Greece, I dreamed that I went to Israel to live on a kibbutz. Waking up, I followed the dream and went to Israel to live on a kibbutz. At an office in Tel Aviv, I was given the options of which kibbutz to live at. One was called Gadot, similar to *Godot,* and for that reason alone (having no other), I chose it.

Of the hundreds of kibbutzim in Israel, Gadot turned out be one of about three that took Christian groups, and after a long and incredible year (which included another jaunt to Europe), I was baptized in the Jordan River. The next day I flew back to America and soon joined the Seventh-day Adventist Church.

About 20 years later (or, just a few months ago) I picked up *Waiting for Godot* and read it again. Though I have encountered some powerful and brilliantly executed polemics against Christianity—even the existence of

God—nothing hit harder than this play. It was the only time since I've been a believer that I felt like a fool for being one.

Waiting for Godot deals with two hapless, homeless men, Vladimir and Estragon, who—living on the side of a road—await this mysterious figure, Godot, who keeps sending them messages with promises to come but, in the end, never does. As they wait, Vladimir and Estragon watch a sad parade of humanity limp, hobble, and stomp past them. Yet even in the midst of anguish, injustice, and sorrow, they cling to their only hope—the hope that Godot will come.

"We'll hang ourselves tomorrow," says Vladimir, "unless Godot comes."

"And if he comes?" responds Estragon.

"We'll be saved."

After finishing the drama, I couldn't imagine how any Christian living (in a sense) on the side of the road couldn't help seeing himself or herself in these two men waiting, and waiting, *and* waiting for Godot.

Beckett wrote the play in 1953; it's now 2000—and, like Vladimir and Estragon, we're waiting (still) for Godot.

Yet one crucial difference exists between our situation and that of Vladimir and Estragon, and it instantly neuters the negative impact of the drama. In *Waiting for Godot* there's no indication that Godot had ever been there; in our situation, "Godot" has, in fact, been here once already—and what He accomplished His first time here guarantees His return. After all, what good was Christ's perfect life, His fulfillment of the demands of the law, and His sacrificial death if He doesn't come back and raise us from the dead? What happened at Christ's first coming assures us of His second, for without the second, the first was futile.

That Christ left us a good example at His first advent is fine, but our situation is too desperate for a mere good example to do us any eternal good. We need a Savior, one who will exchange our mortality for immortality, our corruption for the incorruptible, one who can raise our vile bones and rebreathe life back into the dust upon which we're founded. It was to make all this possible that Jesus came the first time. So unless His life and death were a waste, we have the utter assurance He'll come back and reap the harvest of all that He sowed at His first appearance.

Christ gave Himself as a "ransom for many" (Mark 10:45). Why would He, after having paid such a great price to ransom us, not retrieve what cost Him so much? The reality of the First Coming is the surety of the Second.

Sure, Like Vladimir and Estragon, we're waiting (still) for Godot. Unlike these two poor saps, however, whose hope was never fulfilled, ours was fulfilled already, in the past, at the cross—the utter guarantee that it will, indeed, be consummated in the future.

∽

The Final Fires

In reference to women in Paris feeding birds with pieces of bread "a bit chewed and soggy," the poet Rilke wrote: "It does them good to think that their saliva is getting out in the world a little, that the small birds will fly off with the taste of it in their mouths, even though a moment later they naturally forget it again."

How easy to sulk in our own meaninglessness; to fear that our existence—rank with emotion and fervid imagination within—barely reverberates beyond the smell of our own sweat. A few great ones, the freaks of Providence, might roar across the landscape, their bellows echoing in every corner, but most of us happen and then vanish with as much ado as a dog's dream.

But come on, you're a writer; you write books. Sure, I'm a writer of many out-of-print books, a writer whose fan base is mostly dead. Besides, doesn't Scripture say that one day "the heavens shall pass away with a great noise, and the elements shall melt with fervent heat, the earth also and the works that are therein shall be burned up" (2 Peter 3:10)? And doesn't paper burn a lot faster than earth?

All my books and articles will burn up at the end of the millennium. However depressing that thought, it's not, because it contains the only hope I have that everything about me won't end when this world does.

At death, we can't take anything with us. Even worse, whatever remains after us (books, buildings, a great name, charitable institutions, whatever), the final conflagration will consume. What's left? As far as I can tell, only the characters we form here and souls we've won to the kingdom. Everything else, it seems, is doomed to ultimate oblivion and, therefore, to meaninglessness.

"As I am forgotten/And would be forgotten, so I would forget," wrote T. S. Eliot. What can anything forever gone and forgotten ultimately mean? A billion years from now, who's going to remember *Shrek 2?*

Maybe that's why the Lord uses us to win souls. It's to give us a stake in eternity. In working for the salvation of others, we are already, in a sense, hoeing our ground on the new earth. Winning souls is, perhaps, the best way to lay up treasure in heaven. After all, whatever else we do, if the moths and rust don't get it, the end-time fires will.

Ecclesiastes 3:11 says that God has put *olam,* eternity, in our hearts. There's a longing for eternity that, as mortals, we crave above all else. Getting ourselves, and others, ready for it is about the only way to fulfill that need.

We're told to feed the hungry and clothe the naked; and though the record of those deeds will endure (Matt. 25:38-46), many of those whom we feed and clothe won't; which, in a sense, is why all temporal deeds can dwindle into meaninglessness. Even from a secular perspective, if one day the big bang reverses itself, and the universe collapses into a giant crunch, and we're gone, and every memory or trace of us too, then all that we do—even the good things—are kind of fruitless, anyway.

By the time these words are in print, I'll be 49 years old, probably 60-70 percent of my life gone (too much Häagen-Dazs to lower the percentages). And as I wonder where it has all gone, it's so easy to ask, *How much of what I've done will survive the final fires. (Will I even survive them?) How much of what I have done will be reduced to ashes, even less?*

Life, I always tell my wife, is priorities. We do what's most important; everything else is commentary. It's just that, as Seventh-day Adventists—believing that the world will soon end—our priorities should reflect this fundamental aspect of our faith, which ultimately places everything we do in one of two categories: (1) the acts that endure long past the final fires and (2) those that are as fleeting as the taste of human spit in a bird's mouth.

Is the Universe Friendly?

THIS IS MY FAVORITE section, not because the columns are anything special, but because the topic, the gospel of salvation in Jesus Christ, is. Apart from the amazing truth that the Creator of the universe—the one who filled nothing with the endless expanse of the universe and all that it contains—took upon Himself human flesh and in that flesh bore the corporate woe and pain and sin of our fallen world, what else really matters? That we as sinners can stand, as Ellen White said, "accepted in the Beloved," not because of anything we can do but only because our "defects are covered by the perfection and fullness of the Lord our righteousness" (*Our High Calling,* p. 51) is a truth that should be the focal point, the foundation from which all our other teachings begin. Without this truth, salvation through the imputed righteousness of Jesus, all our other teachings fade into oblivion. The Sabbath, however wonderful, isn't going to save us; only Jesus, through His sacrifice, can. Sabbath might be great, but what a waste of time if we never get to keep one in heaven, and the only way we will is through Jesus' death in our behalf. Hence, the focus is on the great truth of salvation by faith alone.

A Beggar's Prayer

Lord, I approach You this morning with words that, were it not for You, would vanish into oblivion just outside these, my verbal bumblers. That spittle-greased sounds—pumped from a heart that squeezes impure gutturals and other untamed utterances out of these same lips—can reach across the cosmos at speeds that make light stand still is a mystery that science may one day explain. But the other unfathomable mystery beyond formulas and laws is that not only do You hear, but You listen; You care. You respond.

Lord, I'm the stuff of worms; I teeter in the dirt with worms. No matter how many muscles I distend, heaven's far beyond the clouds that float far beyond my grubby reach, which barely gets past the dirt I share with worms, whose bellies would be my postscript but for Your promise to turn this racket of bones into something immortal.

I begin today, Lord, my flesh smelted in sin, my senses fully armed in carnality. Self is cocked, aimed, and ready to unleash seasoned, refined greed. All I can do, in light of the axiom of the evil that's me, is cling to the axiom of goodness and righteousness that's You, that's Yours, that's Christ's, and that's now, by grace, mine.

Lord, help me to experience in the folds of my soul a righteousness that exceeds the evil that rapaciously plucks those witching chords within me; a righteousness hewed into the flesh of the One whose love transcended the pain of a perfection so complete that it fills the world with "the righteousness of God" (Rom. 3:22); a righteousness from heaven that's remolding this moral distortion into the image of a promise that only the Divine can keep.

Lord, I'm a spiritual welfare recipient, an exceeding charity case, taking where I don't give, seeking what I don't deserve, receiving what I don't work for, getting what I don't earn—totally dependent upon the largesse of Another.

And because I have received, help me to give, remembering the grace You've poured out on me so that I can, even if only as tarnished shards, reflect it to others. The gap between what You gave and what I give is as the gap between infinity and finitude. Whatever dribbles of grace I extort from the flesh of my soul toward others can't be measured against the grace You've lavished upon this waxing corpus of greed.

Lord, help me never to forget that no matter who does what to me, he or she and I are still of the same sad ilk, different proportions of one lurid brew, brothers and sisters in sin, fun house reflections of each other's evil. If I were in their slot, I'd probably do the same as they did, if not worse, because I am worse. The distance I cross in order to forgive others is almost nonexistent in contrast to the distance You've crossed in order to forgive me. You, who were in the form of God; You, who thought it not robbery to be equal with God; You, who in order to forgive became of no reputation, took the form of a servant, and in the likeness of humanity were obedient unto death, "even the death of the cross" (Phil. 2:8). That's what it cost You, the Infinite God, to forgive me, a finite mortal.

In contrast, what does it cost me to forgive other finite mortals no worse, if not often better, than I? What does it say about my spiritual poverty that, however cheap, it still bankrupts me to spend it?

Finally, Lord, I thank You that I'm saved by a goodness purified in the soul, refined in the flesh, and shaped in the spirit of Another other than myself, whose pilfered goodness comes in the sporadic drab colors of a mouse. Thank You that the surety of my salvation rests not within these brittle bones or within the boney brine of a soul born and bred amid so much ingrained iniquity that sin was not just what I did but was what I was—and would still be but for the promise made irrefutable in the flesh of Jesus, whose righteousness I can only gawk at in amazement and, in sullied gratitude, nibble at the crumbs.

Amen.

∾

Joshua and the Angel

My wife once described how, as a child, she was taught the "good news" of the judgment.

"Well," she said, "they told us that the judgment is going on in heaven *right now,* which meant that at any moment your name could come up, even if you didn't know when. But if you're not absolutely perfect when it does (you're at the movies or something like that), then your name is blotted out of the book of life, and you are lost. The only trouble is you don't know that you're lost, and although you're still trying to be perfect, it's too late."

How did the "good news" get so good? It's easy. It got that way from *misusing* Ellen White, from taking a few select references (while ignoring everything else that she, not to mention the Bible, says on the topic), and from these few select references constructing an entire theology—no matter how contradictory to the rest of inspiration that theology is.

Every person who joins the Adventist Church ought to be required, before baptism, to read the chapter "Joshua and the Angel" from Ellen White's *Testimonies for the Church,* volume 5, pages 467-476. This section gives a clear, balanced presentation of the pre-Advent judgment and, if read in entirety, would help eliminate the kind of "good news" that my wife and who knows how many others have been "blessed" with all their lives. Because space allows me to extract only a few quotes, and lest I be accused of doing what I have just decried, I say, please read the *entire section* in order to get the *whole picture.*

With Zechariah 3:1-7 as her scriptural basis, White wrote about Joshua, the high priest, "clothed with filthy garments" (verse 3), which represent the sins of God's people. While Joshua is entreating the Angel of the Lord for mercy, "Satan stands up boldly to resist him" (p. 468). She wrote: "The high priest cannot defend himself or his people from Satan's accusations. He does not claim that Israel are free from fault" (p. 468). "The people of God," she said, "have been in many respects very faulty" (p. 474), and "they are fully conscious of the sinfulness of their lives" (p. 473). And Satan, ever the accuser, "points to their filthy garments, their defective characters. He presents their weakness and folly, their sins of ingratitude, their unlikeness to Christ" (p. 473).

How then can these people—who have "defective characters," who have "weakness and folly," and who have been "very faulty"—stand in judgment before a holy God? There's only one way.

"Jesus our Advocate," she wrote, "presents an effectual plea in behalf of all who by repentance and faith have committed the keeping of their souls to Him. He pleads their cause and vanquishes their accuser with the mighty arguments of Calvary" (p. 471). "We cannot," she said, "answer the charges of Satan against us. Christ alone can make an effectual plea in our behalf. He is able to silence the accuser with arguments founded not upon our merits, but on His own" (p. 472).

And precisely because of their wonderful Savior, and because of what He has done for them, these people are "purifying their souls by obeying the truth" (p. 471). They "exert every energy of the soul in the work of overcoming" (p. 472). They are promised that, through "repentance and faith," they can "render obedience to all the commandments of God." And though they have sinned, they have not given themselves over to the control of evil; and, having confessed their sins, they plead "for pardon through Jesus their Advocate" (p. 472).

However much emphasis Ellen White placed on holy living—as did Jesus, Paul, John (Matt. 5:8; Rom. 6:12; 1 John 3:7)—she clearly showed that the foundation of our acceptance with God rests in the "mighty arguments of Calvary" alone, the only way we can be acceptable to a holy God.

"Zechariah's vision of Joshua and the Angel," she wrote, "applies with peculiar force to the experience of God's people in the closing up of the great day of atonement" (p. 472). In other words, in the day of judgment, when our names come up (Luke 12:8; Rev. 3:5), Jesus once and for all stands in our place; His righteousness alone—the only righteousness sufficient to meet the demands of the law—remains as our surety of salvation, now and especially in the pre-Advent judgment.

After all, anything else would hardly be "good news," now, would it?

<hr />

Beyond Logic

We are accepted in the beloved," wrote Ellen White. "The sinner's defects are covered by the perfection and fullness of the Lord our righteousness" (*Our High Calling,* p. 51).

Now, logic alone might have led me (after having read this quote) to think, *Wow, now I can live however I want because my defects are covered by Christ.* Instead, though—in an experience that transcended logic—my thoughts were: *O Lord, thank You so much for this hope! Please cleanse me, change me, purge me of every sin, defilement, and defect. I want to live worthy of the high calling You have given me in Jesus.*

Odd, isn't it, but the more I experience the reality that my "defects are covered by the perfection and fullness of the Lord our righteousness," the more I want to overcome those defects. The more I understand that I am saved by Christ's obedience to the law (as opposed to my own), the more I want to obey that law.

Again, logic would deem the opposite response, wouldn't it? I'm covered, so let's party. And yet the experience of Christ's righteousness covering my sins is exactly what makes me want to purge those sins from my life.

Let me be blunt: I've been an Adventist for almost 23 years now. And after all this time, if there's one thing I am sure of, if there's one thing that I have no question about, if there's one thing that my experience (interpreted and judged by the Word) has taught me, it's this: unless I am saved by a righteousness that exists outside of me, a righteousness that is credited to me independent of my own personal righteousness, then you can stand on that wall at the end of the millennium and wave down to me, because, folks, I'm just not going to be there. It's that simple.

The issues aren't sanctification, or character perfection, or even what's often derided as "demonstration theology" (the idea that God's final generation develops a character that helps answer issues in the great controversy), although I believe in all three concepts. But in the end, however much sanctification, perfection, and character development I possess, unless I am "justified by faith without the deeds of the law" (Rom. 3:28), I'm going to die the second death, because, believe me, I deserve it.

Now, no matter how fundamental this truth is to my walk with the Lord, I'm astounded at the hostility that justification by faith alone arouses among us. No other topic, I've discovered, elicits as angry of a response among the saints as this one. Whenever I write about it, I get barraged with letters, phone calls, e-mails, few of them friendly. In fact, one dear saint (an Adventist minister, to boot) has his own Web site, and when I publish about justification, I get a front-page, mega-pixel haranguing about my promoting cheap grace and an incomplete gospel.

I am baffled, because, unless my whole experience over the past 23 years is wrong, I can't imagine how anyone who knows the Lord, who has even seen a glimpse of God's righteousness as revealed in Jesus, could believe that whatever the Holy Spirit is doing in their lives it's good enough to give them saving merit before God. If, as Ellen White writes, the closer we get to Christ, the worse we seem in our own eyes, then how could anyone drawing near to Jesus believe that whatever is happening in them justifies them in any way? This idea is so alien, so repugnant and antithetical to all that I have experienced over the years, that I'm amazed that people actually believe it.

Without wanting to be judgmental, all I can think is that these folks, having never experienced justification by faith themselves, are allowing logic alone to rule their theology, and logic alone tells them that if we are covered by Christ's righteousness as the only means of salvation, apart from anything that we do or even from anything that is done in us—what's to stop us from living a life of sin?

The answer's easy: "For this is the love of God, that we keep His commandments" (1 John 5:3, NKJV), and nothing will make you love God more than the experience of knowing that your "defects are covered by the perfection and fullness of the Lord our righteousness."

⌒⌒

The Curse of the Law

In *The Spirit of Prophecy* Ellen White wrote: "The law of God could condemn, but could not pardon" (vol. 1, p. 30).

The law could not pardon? Most of us would say we believe that line—but how many will take it to the logical conclusion?

To do so is to believe that no matter how much one proclaims the immutability of the law, or seeks to obey it in spirit and in truth, the law still condemns. It means that Abraham, Moses, Paul, Ellen White—like us—

stand in only one relationship to the law, and that is in condemnation. It is to conclude that there is no pardon, justification, or salvation, but only a curse, guilt, and death in the law.

If the law cannot pardon, then Sabbathkeeping, then not taking the Lord's name in vain, then not lying, then not stealing, then not murdering, then even loving God with all your heart and with all your soul and loving your neighbor as yourself, cannot pardon sin. All they can do, *in and of themselves,* is curse and condemn, because "all who rely on works of the law are under a curse" (Gal. 3:10, RSV).

Notice, Paul didn't write that all who *do* the works of the law are under a curse, for that would contradict many texts regarding God's clear commands for obedience to the law (Rev. 14:12; 22:14; 1 John 5:2, 3; James 2:10); instead he says that those who *rely on* these works for salvation are under the curse—because (as the woman said) "the law of God could condemn, but could not pardon."

Because the law—and works thereof—can only condemn, another means of pardon was necessary, and that was provided by Jesus Christ, who alone met the demands of the law. The law was fulfilled in Jesus in that He met its claims completely, something no one else has done or could ever do. Forgiveness, therefore, can be found only in Jesus, because only His obedience was sufficient for the absolute claims of the law. Jesus alone has what Paul calls "the righteousness of God," the only righteousness that can pardon us, "even the righteousness of God which is by faith of Jesus Christ" (Rom. 3:21, 22).

It has to be only by faith, because our works will never procure the "righteousness of God" for us. It's way too late for the law to do anything except condemn, which is why Paul wrote: "By the works of the law shall no flesh be justified" (Gal. 2:16).

Either salvation is by *faith alone* or it's by works as well. And if it's by works too, then let's take that position to its logical conclusion. If salvation is based *in any way* on our obedience to the law, then God the Son's becoming human flesh, living a life of perfect obedience to the law, and going to the cross, where He faced the Father's wrath against sin, where all the sins of the world fell upon Him, where He became sin for us, where He was judged and condemned in our place, where He died the second death as a substitute for the transgressions of the whole world—*all that still wasn't good enough?* It wasn't sufficient to pardon us? It was lacking something that can be made up by our "works of the law"? Please! And yet that's the only logical conclusion of any theology that attributes merit to lawkeeping. It's like trying to make Bill Gates richer by hurling cow dung into his bank account.

E. J. Waggoner, in *The Glad Tidings,* wrote: "People take the sign for the substance, the end for the means. They see that righteousness reveals itself in good works. Therefore they assume that the good works bring the righteousness" (p. 53).

They're wrong. Good works, "the works of the law," are the personal manifestations of a person who has been born again; works are the outward, subjective expression of a life changed by "the righteousness of God which is by the faith of Jesus Christ." But they can never, under any circumstances, save us; on the contrary, all they can do, *in and of themselves,* is kill us—because again, as the prophet said, "the law of God could condemn, but could not pardon."

Special Relativity and the Cross

Scripture says, "God is light" (1 John 1:5); a metaphor, obviously. About two millennia later Albert Einstein helped reveal what that metaphor means.

If Frank is standing still, and a train approaches him at 100 kilometers per hour, Frank and the moving train will meet at, of course, 100 kilometers per hour. If Frank runs toward the moving train at 20 kilometers per hour, Frank and the train will meet at 120 kilometers per hour. If Frank runs at 20 kilometers per hour in the same direction that the train is moving (at 100 kilometers per hour), Frank and the train will meet at 80 kilometers per hour as the train passes him. Pure classical physics, pure common sense, nothing more.

If Frank is, again, standing still, and a beam of light approaches him at 300,000 kilometers per second (kps), it will reach him at 300,000 kps. If Frank moves toward that beam of light at 100,000 kps, then that beam will reach him at . . . 400,000 kps, right? The light is moving at 300,000 kps toward Frank, Frank's moving at 100,000 kps toward it, and 100,000 plus 300,000 equals 400,000. What could be simpler?

Only one problem, the answer is wrong. The beam of light will still reach

Frank at 300,000 kps. If he were moving at 299,000 kps toward the light, or 299,000 kps away from it, there would be no difference. The light will reach him always—no matter his speed relative to it—at the same rate, 300,000 kps.

But that's impossible. If Frank moves toward or away from something moving in his direction, the speed at which he meets it would be determined by the speed at which he's moving either toward or away from it, as with the train. Right?

Wrong, at least with light. Whenever anyone takes a measurement of the velocity of light, regardless of that person's constant motion relative to the light (either toward or away from it), the light will always reach that person at the same rate.

How could that be? The answer—formulated by Albert Einstein in 1905 and later verified with awesome accuracy—is that *time itself* slows down the faster one moves, and it does so in a proportional manner that always makes light approach its target at 300,000 kps. Though Frank is moving at 100,000 kilometers per second toward (or away from) the beam of light, a second for him (at his speed) slows down enough to ensure that the beam of light will reach him at 300,000 kps.

This change isn't in the clock, as if speed did something to the gears, cranks, and dials; it's much more fundamental. Time itself, and thus all that happens within time—such as the functions of Frank's brain, the beat of his heart, the blink of his eye, and the tick of his watch—slow down because *time itself* has slowed down. This is Einstein's Special Theory of Relativity, and it says that no matter how fast we move toward light or flee from it, light always reaches us at the same speed.

Now, if "God is light," could this mean that no matter how fast we are moving, either toward or away from Him, God and His love remain constant toward us? Could this mean that at the cross Christ's death and the love that His death expressed for the world never varies, no matter how quickly we are moving toward, or fleeing from, Him? Could it mean, as Ty Gibson wrote in *Seeing With New Eyes,* that God's love "is a constant, immovable reality not dependent on our goodness"? Could it mean that because of the cross, where Christ paid the penalty for the sins of every human being, His love for every human being—even those who spurn that love and are lost—never wavers, never fluctuates, never varies, regardless of our position relative to it; but like light remains constant, even if all other reality, including time itself, has to be bent and twisted in order to accommodate God's invariant love toward us?

Of course it does.

As Scripture says, "Every good gift and every perfect gift is from above, and cometh down from *the Father of lights, with whom is no variableness, neither shadow of turning*" (James 1:17).

No kidding.

$$\sim$$

Anniversary

Twenty years ago this spring one of the greatest things that could ever happen happened—to me: after a dramatic new-birth experience I joined the Seventh-day Adventist Church. (Only those who have lived without belief in God, without hope of answers, and without the promise of anything ultimate other than rigor mortis and worms can know what I mean.)

Looking back, though, can be painful, for the view over my shoulder is littered with mistakes, failures, and sins left in my wake.

Martin Weber (my former pastor before he moved west) used to say, "Cliff Goldstein is living proof that sanctification is the work of a lifetime." Maybe—but only if I live as long as Methuselah. Victories that I should have had long ago have been more distant than faint galaxies; spiritual goals seem as unreachable as childhood fantasies; promises made to myself have turned out to be lies to myself. I do things now I might not have once done, rationalizing my actions in the name of *spiritual maturity* or (even more a joke) *freedom in the gospel.* Though Jesus is supposed to be my example, why do I still relate so much better to Judas?

Intellectually I've never been more convinced of the Adventist message, especially because I see how either barren and/or unbiblical the alternatives are. My brain has had plenty of time to grow synapses tightly around our core beliefs, which I accept with the kind of certitude usually reserved only for algebraic or geometric equations.

No, the problem isn't my mind but my heart, which has grown cold in comparison to those earliest days when my faith burned with a sacred fire that revealed much more heat than light. (I still remember, after my first study on Rome and America's end-time alliance, walking on the campus of the University of Florida and telling people I could prove—*from*

74

Scripture!—that Ted Kennedy was going to be the next president of the United States.) Today, after 20 years in the church, 17 of them in the Big House (the General Conference), I wish I could trade some of this light for some of that heat.

Writing, in a sense, is my salvation; my books do me more good than anyone else, not that many read them anymore (as my dwindling royalty statements prove). The one fear I have about traveling is that the rare precious souls who do read my words will, after meeting me in the flesh, think, *What a dweeb!* Those who work here and know me aren't in danger of such disappointments.

Perhaps my only progress is that I'm so much more accepting of others now, and so much less inclined to judge or condemn. I have learned to love and respect those who differ with me, *even theologically*—a radical change from 20, even 10, years ago. But then again, I wonder, *Does this acceptance reflect spiritual maturity, or the dimming of the fire?*

Yet, amid all this spiritual angst, I'm not discouraged, because my situation forces me every day back to Jesus and the cross. In Christ, who "gave himself for me" (Gal. 2:20), I find the only reason I have to keep going, even enthusiastically, because I can claim, by faith, His perfections in place of my own gross imperfections. Through Christ, God views me (despite my defects) as righteous—and, in the end, God's view is the only one that matters. Without this wonderful, hopeful gospel promise, I'd have to have been a masochistic fool not to have given up long ago.

Instead, I said to myself, "Either I believe God's promises of forgiveness or I don't. Either I believe that God accepts me in Christ, because of His righteousness, not mine, or I don't. Either I believe that 'if any man sin, we have an advocate with the Father, Jesus Christ' [1 John 2:1], or I don't. Either I believe the promise (the hardest one of all) that 'he which hath begun a good work in you will perform it until the day of Jesus Christ' [Phil. 1:6] or I don't."

But I do, which is why, despite the sins, failings, and mistakes strewn along them, the past 20 years have been my best yet.

Rigid Satisfaction

Dictated by the blind poet near the end of his life, John Milton's *Paradise Lost* has to be one of history's greatest spiritual and literary coups. Though agreeing with Samuel Johnson that "none ever wished it longer," and despite its few excruciating errors (such as having Satan already in hell), while reading the poem I had to avoid the temptation to read it for worship. At times the work seemed "inspired," whatever exactly that means. . . .

For starters, *Paradise Lost* runs riot with the great controversy theme. From beginning to end Satan fulminates against the God who threw him and his rebellious angels out of heaven ("Him the Almighty Power/Hurled headlong flaming from th' ethereal sky"). Unable to take back heaven, "th' Arch-Fiend" determined to destroy man on earth instead. The gist of the poem relates him seeking to do just that.

Besides the great controversy theme, Milton unpacks the crucial question of free will. He has God saying:

> Freely they stood who stood, and fell who fell.
> Not free, what proof could they have giv'n
>   sincere
> Of true allegiance, constant faith
>   or love,
> Where only what they needs must
>   do, appeared,
> Not what they would? What praise
>   could they receive?
> What pleasure I from such
>   obedience paid. . . .

And even though God knew beforehand that they would sin, "Foreknowledge had no influence on their fault,/Which had no less prov'd certain unforeknown." In other words, regardless of what God knew beforehand, free beings fell of their own free choice. Foreknowledge foreordained nothing, especially the Fall.

For me, the most "inspired" part of Milton's amazing achievement was his theology of the cross, his unambiguous explanation of the atonement, of the Son of God paying in His own flesh the divine penalty for human transgression.

In the following lines he has the Father laying out the principle of the great substitution. Talking about the fallen Adam (and hence fallen humanity), He says to the heavenly host:

> Die he or justice must; unless for him
> Some other able, and as willing, pay
> The rigid satisfaction, death for death.

Who, of course, could pay that "rigid satisfaction" other than the Son of God Himself? Here, speaking to the Father, the Son says:

> Behold me then: me for him, life for life
> I offer: on me let thine anger fall;
> Account me man; I for his sake will leave
> Thy bosom, and this glory next to thee
> Freely put off, and for him lastly die.

And the Father later replies:

> . . . So man, as is most just,
> Shall satisfy for man, be judged and die,
> And dying rise, and rising with him raise
> His brethren, ransomed with his own dear life.

What a concise and powerful rendition of salvation, of what Christ has done for us by taking upon Himself "thine anger"—God's righteous judgment against sin and iniquity so that instead of this anger falling on us for our lies, our lusts, our deceptions and greed and avarice—it all fell on Jesus Christ. Jesus covered the debt; all that was owed God in order to satisfy divine justice was paid at the cross. Nothing adds to the payment; nothing diminishes it. All we can do is hang our helpless souls before the provision and claim it for ourselves. Or, as Milton so eloquently expressed it: "His crime makes guilty all his sons; thy merit,/Imputed, shall absolve them who renounce/Their own both righteousness and unrighteous deeds,/And live in thee transplanted."

This poem reveals the work of the Holy Spirit funneled through a human channel endowed with remarkable literary gifts. Some say that Ellen White had read, and was influenced by, *Paradise Lost*. If so, I say only, "Amen!" She knew, obviously, what source she was drinking from.

⟨∾⟩

Is the Universe Friendly?

I admit to the moments—moments of spiritual malaise when my soul feels vacuumed of everything except earthiness; when the spiritual feels more chemical than empyreal; and when the words of T. S. Eliot— "We are the hollow men/We are the stuffed men/Leaning together/Head-piece filled with straw"—sum up my religious experience quite accurately.

We all (I assume) have hobbled through such times when the contrast between what we are and should be crushes faith; if not so much in God but in the hope of ever seeing Him, except maybe from a distance, on a vast plane, along with the rest of Gog and Magog (Rev. 20:8).

Again and again, though, a thought comes to my rescue, a revealed truth that better than anything else frees me from the shackles of self.

It starts with John, who, talking about Jesus, says: "All things were made by him; and without him was not any thing made that was made" (John 1:3). Without Jesus nothing made was made; not time, not space, not even the vibrating strings that some scientists now theorize compose all matter (a string is to the size of a proton as a proton is to the solar system). Galaxies, goats, black holes, water, dark matter, antimatter, electro-magnetism, DNA, the inverse square law, square roots, even the square itself—all things "were made by him," at least all things that "were made," and what existing wasn't made except God?

Then I contrast this thought, that of Jesus having made "all things," with another revealed truth: "And Jacob begat Joseph the husband of Mary, of whom was born Jesus, who is called Christ" (Matt. 1:16).

Think about it: the power that created "all things," the universe, that power "shrank down" and became a human being; and not just any human being—but Jesus of Nazareth? Come on! The Jesus we see in the Gospels, hungry, weeping, scorned, and finally crucified, was the Creator of the universe, the One without whom "was not any thing made that was made"? Who can grasp this? The idea is so audacious, so outlandish that it defies the imagination (which just shows how limited imaginations are). How dare we think that as human beings we could be so worthwhile in the eyes of God that He would do this for us?

A philosopher once asked, "Is the universe friendly?" If a pure chance creation, then no—it's hostile, filled with cold and uncaring laws that never apologize, that never listen to a child's cry or a parent's plea. But if, as the Bible teaches, this universe was created by a God who has linked Himself to us in such an intimate way, who has bridged the vast gulf between us and Him through the agony of the cross, then the answer is yes, the universe is friendly beyond anything rationality can comprehend.

There's something about that thought; that of the Creator of the universe coming down, not just into humanity, but as Jesus, with the predetermined plan (Rev. 13:8) to die for our sins. That idea overwhelms all others; it becomes the focus, the pivot point through which everything else should be viewed, judged, and understood. The cross reconfigures reality, rewrites axioms, changes equations.

General relativity shows that gravity, which pervades the whole universe, is nothing but matter bending space and time; the cross shows that they're bent into the shape of a loving, longing smile.

If you believe that the Creator of the universe, the One who made "everything that was made," morphed into Jesus of Nazareth and freely offered Himself to die a cruel death all in order to give us eternal life . . . what else matters? What else could matter? Everything is kind of swept away, kind of anyway . . . including my own sense of spiritual failure. Before the cross, and the incredible view of reality it offers, even I, hollow man that I am, rejoice in a hope that's still hard for me to understand; a hope that I have to take on faith, for nothing else can reach far enough to grasp it.

·∾·

The
Christless Cross

An independent ministry published a while back a special issue of its flagship magazine. Having not read the publication in years and thinking that, perhaps, the editors have (like the rest of us sinners) mellowed over time, I decided to give this new issue a fair, serious read, particularly the article entitled "The Three Angels' Messages," because I was curious as to how it tackled the first angel's "everlasting gospel."

To my dispirited disappointment, its definition of the everlasting gospel was that "every man, woman and child must die daily. We must surrender our will moment by moment to God—the heart united with His heart, the mind united with His mind—only then can we think the thoughts and live the life of Jesus."

Here we are in the twenty-first century, more than 113 years after 1888—and this is how some *still* define the everlasting gospel? Isn't the everlasting gospel the good news that Jesus, the God-man, lived a life of perfect obedience to the law and then died as my substitute in order that I, by faith, can claim His perfect righteousness as my own, a righteousness that comes only by faith in His righteousness—a righteousness credited to me apart from "the works of the law" (Gal. 2:16)?

Now, I'm not one of those who deem it necessary to limit the gospel to justification alone. The first angel's message itself includes, under the rubric of the everlasting gospel the judgment as well (Rev. 14:7), so we who profess faith in the gospel should be at least as inclusive. Through the power of God's Spirit a believer can, indeed, die to self daily and, indeed, think the thoughts and live the life of Jesus. That's good news too. But the moment these internal actions become *conditions* for justification, the moment they become the *means* by which a person is saved, the good news gets blunted—like with a sledge hammer.

Although the magazine's editors would be shocked to realize it, its theology is just like Roman Catholicism, which teaches that an infused righteousness—a righteousness that inheres within—helps justify a sinner. In Roman Catholic theology righteousness is mediated through the church and its sacraments, but both theologies end up in the same place: justification depends upon personal, internal perfection, a rather depressing prospect for even the most sanctified saint. Rome, understanding this problem, has at least given its people some hope: it's called purgatory (these folks don't even offer that).

Notice how humanistic, how sinner-centered, this understanding of the gospel is. We must die daily, we must surrender our will, we must do this, we must do that. The argument that it's God doing the works in us, and thus not our own, doesn't let them off the hook. God doesn't force Himself upon us, or into us. If some folks do good works and some don't, it's only because some have made a choice to allow God to work in them and some haven't. It's still the people, themselves, doing these works, and if these works justify them, then they're saved by faith and works, period.

God does work in us so that we can become righteous; that's an undeniable part of the Christian experience. But no matter how righteous we become by what God does in us, our salvation still comes *only* from what God has done outside us, in the life and death of Jesus (see Phil. 3:9). Our hope of salvation must never remain centered upon ourselves, or what happens within; instead, the righteousness that saves us—the obedience that redeems us—and the holiness that justifies us—always remains external to us, a righteousness that exists in heaven itself, "the righteousness of God" Himself (Rom. 3:21).

It's too bad about that magazine. When some Adventists are trying to meld evolution with our faith, these people aren't; when some Adventists are questioning our prophetic message, these people aren't; when some Adventists are buying into the subjective and secularist-premised notions of historical criticism, these people aren't; when some Adventists are doubting the prophetic ministry of Ellen White, these people aren't.

All of which is commendable, except for one technicality: there's no Christ on their cross, which means that whatever good they offer comes burdened with the unbearable weight of salvation by works, which is no gospel and, certainly, not the "everlasting" one.

—∽—

To Know God

If the double helices of my DNA were ever stretched out in flat, parallel lines, no base clefs, c-minors, or chords would dangle from the rungs. I can't sing, can't hold a tune, am rhythmically dysfunctional, and (except for occasionally flapping my ears to old Led Zeppelin or Pink Floyd tunes belching from the car radio) I rarely listen to music. It just, frankly, bores me.

The other day, though, a snippet from some Christian ditty roused the comatose soloist within me. "I believe in You, Lord," the gospel singer sang, "but do I know You?"

Wow! What a profound question, what an incisive distinction, because knowing God isn't just believing propositional truths about Him. The most unrepentant degenerate can believe in God's eternal nature, His creative power, even His atoning death. But that's no more knowing God than if Adam's knowing Eve, in Genesis 4:1, was limited to seeing her unclothed.

What does it mean, then, to know the Lord? To know that 3 + 3 = 6, or to know that matter bends space and time, or to know that Jesus is the Savior of the world, is one thing. But to *know* the Lord? The verb here takes on another meaning entirely.

That's why devotion, prayer, and Bible study, however necessary for knowing the Lord, aren't sufficient. Having a relationship with God isn't synonymous with knowing Him, either—after all, I have a relationship with Osama bin Laden, yet I don't know him. Everyone, whether they realize it or not, exists in a relationship with God, somewhat in the same way we all exist in a relationship with the sun (some just have more light than do others).

Knowing God is more than an intellectual, emotional, or spiritual state. Knowing God is, instead, what we do; it's how we live. "And hereby we do know that we know him, if we keep his commandments. He that saith, I know him, and keepeth not his commandments, is a liar, and the truth is not in him" (1 John 2:3, 4). The keeping of the commandments is the way we know God; it's the knowledge of God made manifest, given flesh, blood, and breath; it's the knowledge of God unfurled in words, deeds, and motives. Obedience doesn't merely reveal that we know the Lord; instead, obedience—not in the stale, lifeless letter of the law but in the freedom of already having been forgiven in Christ—*is how we come to know Him.* We know God by obeying Him. We can master theology, memorize texts, expound on the minutiae of forensic and imparted righteousness, but without obedience, we don't know the Lord.

"He judged the cause of the poor and needy; then it was well with him: was not this to know me? saith the Lord" (Jer. 22:16). Was not *what* to "know me"? It was to judge the cause of the poor and the needy; it was doing good, the giving of oneself for the good of others. A life of self-sacrifice, of disinterested love while seeking nothing in return, that's the essence of obeying the law—and, even more so, that's the essence of knowing God.

"He that loveth not knoweth not God; for God is love" (1 John 4:8). Who hasn't experienced how selfless devotion for others, even if only in infrequent spasms, draws us closer to our God, revealing Him and His character to us in ways that nothing else can?

So the question *I believe in You, Lord, but do I know You?* pummeled me, and I answered, Yes, I know the Lord, but only enough to know my need to repent for all that I am (but shouldn't be), for all that I am not (but ought to be). And that deed—in which I confess my sins and then plead for a righteousness that exists outside of me, a righteousness that I have no claim to other than my great need—helps me to know, even better, my loving, forgiving, and pardoning God, who says that "if we confess our sins, he is faithful and just to forgive us our sins, and to cleanse us from all unrighteousness" (1 John 1:9)—a promise that's music to my ears.

No. It's so much better than that.

─◯─

Self-delusion

Every idea, image, sound, and touch you've ever felt, heard, seen, or thought, you've done so in warm-blooded darkness. Our character, emotions, knowledge, passions, and dreams foment in a realm where light never reaches, because our mind—where almost all that we are is—sits locked in a box that lets no light in. We are, literally, in darkness, and I see this darkness as a metaphor for self-delusion.

I've met people—bright, educated people, even vegetarian, Sabbathkeeping people—who were so self-deluded, so skewed and imbalanced in their own view of themselves and their relationship to reality, that they seemed to exist in a parallel (or maybe perpendicular?) universe. Facts of sterile clarity, after being processed in their minds, would come out so differently from what seemed to go in that I'd have to rub my eyes just to make sure we're looking at the same thing. Years ago, after listening to some poor soul express a view of himself that fit reality like panty hose on a lobster, I was hit by the fearful thought *What about me? How self-deluded am I?*

We all, I imagine, to some degree are. We have to be. Socrates once said, "Know thyself." Most people who do so become suicidal. "Man," wrote Joseph Brodsky, "is more frightening than his skeleton." That, I think, explains our capacity for self-delusion; it's a kind of defense mechanism, a soiled way of deflecting ourselves from ourselves. It's bad enough to see another's degeneracy; who can bear the sight of his or her own? Our most effective masks are the ones that we wear outside in.

"How canst thou say, I am not polluted, I have not gone after Baalim?" (Jer. 2:23) the Lord asks those who have so long been defiled and who have so long gone after "Baalim" that they see themselves as doing neither. Judas, Ellen White wrote, actually thought he was doing good by betraying Jesus. The Laodicean disease is, essentially, self-delusion: "Because thou sayest, I am rich, and increased with goods, and have need of nothing; and knowest not that thou art wretched, and miserable, and poor, and blind, and naked" (Rev. 3:17). And then there's the most frightful self-delusion, the self-delusion of the damned: "Lord, Lord, have we not prophesied in thy name? . . . And then will I profess unto them, I never knew you: depart from me, ye that work iniquity" (Matt. 7:22, 23).

The only cure is the cross—rather ironic because the cross is what shows us just how bad we are, and it's our own sick visage that causes us to hide behind self-delusion in the first place. Yet the cross also shows us that no matter how wretched we are, God accepts us anyway. At the cross we can afford to look at ourselves because whatever appears has been covered by the blood of Jesus, and it's only when we know we've been covered that we dare take off our own masks. What does it matter what we think about ourselves as long as we know what God thinks? "For if our heart condemn us, God is greater than our heart, and knoweth all things" (1 John 3:20). Only when we know what God thinks about us can we start stripping away the lies in which we've hidden ourselves; only as we know that we are accepted and loved can we have the security to look squarely in the mirror and confront the evil that looks back.

Otherwise, how will we overcome sins that we don't see? In the sure refuge of salvation, where we have been accepted in Jesus despite our sins, we can begin the long, painful, and arduous processes of having those sins, nerve ending by nerve ending, purged from our lives. If not, sin will only increase our self-delusion, and we will compose myth upon myth that will push us deeper into the dark and mazy rills of our sin-wearied mind, where we will wander farther and farther away from the One who said, "I am come a light into the world, that whosoever believeth on me should not abide in darkness" (John 12:46).

～

1888 and
All That . . .

While reading the four-volume *Ellen G. White 1888 Materials,* I noticed a sharp contrast between Ellen White's theology regarding 1888 and the so-called "1888 message." Almost nothing in this compilation (or, in fact, in any of her writing) expresses what some claim Jones and Waggoner had taught at the 1888 General Conference session. Because Ellen White claimed that she had been teaching for "forty-five years" (*Manuscript Releases,* vol. 1, p. 142) the same message as Jones and Waggoner presented at that session, the absence of "1888 message" theology in her writings reveals that whatever was preached in 1888—it wasn't "the 1888 message."

Those promoting this specific message claim that the entire world, every human being, had been legally justified at the cross. Even before we profess faith in Christ (even before we ever heard of Him) our sins were legally forgiven before God. Before we claim justification, we are legally justified; before we claim salvation, we are legally saved. Faith doesn't change our status; it simply acknowledges what that status had always been. Then, as a result of acknowledging what Christ has done for us, we follow the Lord in faith and obedience. This personal acknowledgment leads to what seems to be a "second justification" (what they call "justification by faith"). As long as we do not reject what Christ has done for us, we remain saved. In this view, in fact, it's easy to be saved and hard to be lost.

However assuring, this theology distorts the universality of what happened at Calvary. Yes, Christ tasted "death for every man" (Heb. 2:9); yes, God was in Christ, "reconciling the world unto himself" (2 Cor. 5:19). But this does not mean we were all saved, unconditionally, at the cross; it means that at the cross Christ bore the condemnation of the world's sin, and thus anyone who claims, by faith, what Christ did becomes legally justified in the sight of God (hence the phrase "justification by faith"). The good news, a message full of assurance, is that by faith alone, and not by works of the law, we can stand before God in the perfection and righteousness of Christ. "But to him that worketh not, but believeth on him that justifieth the ungodly, his faith is counted for righteousness" (Rom. 4:5).

Though there's no space here to debate these differing positions from the Bible, I reiterate the issue posed above: Ellen White said that the "most precious message" of Jones and Waggoner (*1888 Materials,* p. 1336) was "old light" (*Selected Messages,* book 3, p. 168), something that she had been preaching for decades. Yet nothing in her writing teaches universal, legal justification, as do proponents of the 1888 message. I'm not talking about a garnered sentence hither and yon; anyone can prove anything from her writings that way. Instead (and I ask in all sincerity), If this was such an important message, why in all of Ellen White's writings does no book, no chapter in a book, no article, or even a simple full paragraph spell, out in unambiguous and systematic terms the idea of universal legal justification prior to personal faith? One would think, for example, that *Steps to Christ,* written in response to the 1888 session, would—in all its simple and lucid pages—have expressed something of this theology, and yet there's nothing, an absence that seriously undermines the credibility of the 1888 message.

Now, I expect a barrage of hot letters accusing me of all manner of perfidy and concupiscence; what I don't expect, however, is something clear and systematic from Ellen White promoting this theology, and that's because it's not there. Which leads, again, to this fundamental dilemma: Ellen White said that what Jones and Waggoner preached in 1888 was what she had been preaching for 40 years. Those promoting the 1888 message claim to be teaching what Jones and Waggoner had preached in 1888. Yet Ellen White doesn't teach the 1888 message. What conclusion can one draw, therefore, other than that the 1888 message isn't the message given in 1888?

Thus, as a church, whatever our faults, we're not guilty today of rejecting the gospel simply because we reject what some call the 1888 message.

On the contrary, it's hard to see how that message could be the gospel, at least as the prophet understood it.

‿

The Wages of (Forgiven) Sin

An ordained Adventist minister wept in my office like an abandoned child: his wife, as a 12-year-old, had been sexually molested by her father, and 20 years later the abused little girl had crumbled into an emotionally destroyed woman whose pain brought the walls of her home down upon her husband and their three children.

Though I have no reason to believe that it ended this way—suppose her father had repented? Suppose he was convicted by the Spirit of his sin, that he dropped to his knees, confessed, and with acid tears pleaded with Jesus for pardon? Would he be forgiven?

Be careful what you reply, because if you answer "Yes," you're saying that this man—who maybe minutes before was having sexual intercourse with his little girl—was now *perfect in Christ*. You're saying that his heinous sin was pardoned by the blood of the Lamb, and the man stood clothed in a heavenly righteousness, "even the righteousness of God which is by faith of Jesus Christ unto all and upon all them that believe" (Rom. 3:22).

Are you prepared to say so? What other choice do you have? Where sin abounds, grace does more abound, right? Pardon to the chief of sinners, right? Christ died for the ungodly, right?

Yet, even with this answer, there's another side to this equation, one not generally talked about.

After years of wandering in a wasteland of legalism, which has left untold thousands of souls spiritually shipwrecked on the shoals of guilt and hopelessness, the Adventist Church is finally understanding the gospel, understanding that redemption is not something that happens *in us* but something that happened *for us* in Jesus. Our redemption is not in ourselves, but in Christ: "Being justified freely by his grace through *the redemption that is in Christ Jesus*" (verse 24). In Him we have been redeemed; in Him, and Him alone, is our redemption. Redemption has never been, nor even is now, in ourselves; it happens, and exists, only in Christ. This is the essence of the gospel, the essence of the good news, the essence of assurance that so many Adventists seem to crave.

Yet, in our quest for "assurance of salvation," have we forgotten how many millions of lives have been ruined or made unbearably difficult by sins that have already been forgiven? Have we been so obsessed with what happens to the record of our sins in heaven that we have ignored the record of them on earth, the record that's painfully etched in our own beings and the beings of those whom we love; a record that's not so quickly wiped clean? How nice, indeed, if relief from the *consequences* of our sins could come as quickly as the *pardon* for them does.

Scripture drips with examples of the devastation wrought by forgiven sin, pardoned sin, like David, who, though immediately forgiven for adultery, murder, and treachery (after he repented), still had to live with the bitter consequences. Sure, his sin had been covered by the blood of Christ, and in the book of record "pardon" had been written in nice big letters next to those sins. David understood justification by faith; anyone who could write Psalm 51 had to. Our problem isn't the legal, forensic declaration of pardon in heaven but suffering the consequences of those legally and forensically pardoned sins here on earth.

God is a merciful God. He can and He does bring healing. But it's often a long, laborious, and painful process. And besides, even healed wounds leave scars. . . .

Maybe it's time we stop our navel-gazing, obsession with "assurance" and instead seek power on high for victory over the sins that so often cause us to question our salvation to begin with—sins that always one way or another, in one manifestation or another, bear bad consequences, not just for sinners but for the unfortunate beings who share the planet with them.

The Owl of Minerva

AS ADVENTISTS, WE'VE always been interested in prophecy, and for a number of reasons, one of them being that we see ourselves—and rightly so—as a prophetic movement. Prophecy plays a crucial role in Scripture, too; after all, both of Jesus' comings were foretold in prophecy. Prophecy also forms the template for our worldview; it gives us a background to interpret current events. But interpreting current events through our prophet lens can be a tricky venture, to say the least, which is why this section—besides doing a little of that—also looks at the prophecies themselves and how we interpret them. This is important because we face today not just challenges to our interpretation of events, but challenges to our whole prophetic framework. For better or for worse, these pages attempt to answer the challenges, showing (I hope) just how solid a biblical foundation we have for what we believe.

Being or Nothingness

Though barely worth the effort, I just finished plodding through Jean-Paul Sartre's 800-some page tome *Being and Nothingness,* a "phenomenological essay on ontology"—essentially Sartre's attempt to understand "what must man be and the world be in order for a relation between them to be possible." Toward the end of the book (considered "the Bible of existentialism") Sartre did write something incredibly profound. He said that ultimately "the best way to conceive of the fundamental project of human reality is to say that man is a being whose project is to be God. . . . Or if you prefer, man fundamentally has the desire to be God."

How fascinating that the century's most influential atheist would so cogently capture such a basic theological truth.

"You have said in your heart: 'I will ascend into heaven, I will exalt my throne above the stars of God; I will also sit on the mount of the congregation on the farthest sides of the north: I will ascend above the heights of the clouds, *I will be like the Most High'*" (Isa. 14:13, 14, NKJV).

"Son of man, say to the prince of Tyrus, Thus saith the Lord God; Because thine heart is lifted up, and thou hast said, *I am a God,* I sit in the seat of God in the midst of the seas; yet thou art a man, and not God, though thou set thine heart as the heart of God. . . . Therefore thus saith the Lord God; Because *thou hast set thine heart as the heart of God"* (Eze. 28:2-6).

This same desire brought Eve's downfall as well. Lucifer didn't tempt her with promises of riches, fame, or sensual pleasure; instead, he used the same thing that did him in: the desire, as Sartre said, to be like God. When the serpent told Eve that "you will be like God" (Gen. 3:5, NKJV), she took the bait, because apparently something inside her wanted to be "like God."

It didn't end in Eden, either. Paul described the essential characteristic of the antichrist in terms similar to Sartre's: "Let no man deceive you by any means: for that day shall not come, except there come a falling away first, and that man of sin be revealed, the son of perdition; who opposeth and exalteth himself above all that is called God, or that is worshipped; so that he as God sitteth in the temple of God, *shewing himself that he is God*" (2 Thess. 2:3, 4).

No wonder theologian Reinhold Niebuhr wrote, "The sin of man is that he seeks to make himself God."

What is it about the creature, then, that wants to be the Creator? Though most of us don't, at least consciously, think that we want to be God, the issue is manifested much more subtly than that. Satan, Eve, the "son of perdition"—all were seeking an authority other than the Lord, namely, themselves. Since God is the sovereign of the universe, and His essential role is to rule, to make oneself the final authority, to set oneself and one's own particular views as the ultimate standard, is essentially to try to make oneself God.

Whenever we take prerogatives on ourselves that belong only to God—such as ignoring a day that God has set aside as holy and keeping instead one of human choosing—we are making ourselves out to be God. Though he came at it from a totally different perspective, Sartre's philosophy led him to understand what is essentially the *original* original sin.

The great controversy between Christ and antichrist in the last days will climax around this fundamental issue. Do we follow the Lord and let Him be God, or do we make ourselves the final authority, and thus become our own gods? Will we obey God's commands or those of another one?

No matter how big the universe might appear, there's room for only one God, which means that sooner or later all the false gods—even those made of bone and wrapped in sinew and flesh and able to act rationally—must go. And though Sartre's use of the terms was radically different, the choice we make here about who will ultimately be God will determine our fate, which will truly be either "being" or "nothingness."

‑‑‑

The Owl
of Minerva

C reationists, flat-earthers, and bigots," wrote law professor Ronald Dworkin, "are ridiculed in many parts of America."

The context of this quote isn't important; the grouping of creationists with bigots and flat-earthers is. And here's why: However much liberal Christianity likes to present itself as a valiant and courageous attempt to be progressive, to keep up with the times, and to break away from the shackles of fundamentalism or staid tradition, the truth is that courage is needed, not to keep up with the times—but to defy them.

How much intellectual courage, for instance, does it take in the twentieth century to believe in evolution or higher criticism or moral relativism? It takes none, because these are in vogue—and since when has it taken guts to be in vogue?

It's also crucial to notice that these Christians are embracing, not Baal worship, child-sacrifice, or polytheism (the things that gave our spiritual ancestors so much trouble), but evolution, higher criticism, and relativism; because these (not polytheism and Baal worship) are the trends. And if this present world should last 100 more years, our progeny will smile at these trends then as we do Baal worship, an earth-centered universe, and bell-bottoms now.

"Take heed to yourselves, that your heart be not deceived, and ye turn aside, and serve other gods, and worship them" (Deut. 11:16). The word for "deceived" means literally "open." Thus it could read, "Take heed to yourselves, that your heart be not *opened,* and ye turn aside."

Of course, it's so difficult, even for Christians, to view the world apart from our own culture and time. It's like trying to take off your Nikes while jogging. "The owl of Minerva," wrote Hegel, "spreads its wings only with the falling of the dusk," meaning that only in hindsight, only from a position of looking back, can we really get a more objective view of reality. How imperative, therefore, in our attempt to be relevant, that we carefully sift through the current moral, scientific, and theological spasms of our times and culture before making them our own.

As Seventh-day Adventists, fortunately, we have a chance, in a sense, to step out of our time and culture and look back, because we believe in the Bible. And the Scriptures take us to the true "end of history," to the final consummation of the world, and allow us from that perspective to view our times now.

Last-day prophecies tell us that a massive deception of pandemic proportions will sweep the world, and that only a small, despised remnant—who refuse to follow the trends, who have the courage to defy the times, a group depicted as those who "keep the commandments of God, and have the testimony of Jesus Christ" (Rev. 12:17)—will stand; while the whole world, following worldly trends, will "worship the beast and his image" (Rev. 14:11).

What the Bible and Ellen White tell us about final events should help us put our own time in perspective. They should make us realize that one of the most dangerous things is to open our hearts to the many trends and currents in which we find ourselves immersed, and which seem so logical, right, and true at the moment, but are discarded as myths by the next generation and, even worse, are viewed by God as fables, "vain jangling" (1 Tim. 1:6), and deceit.

Our understanding of the end of world should tell us that we must cling to truth with all our heart, soul, and mind, because only a love of truth will enable us to stand when overwhelming moral, logical, intellectual, and spiritual arguments and appeals will be directed against all that we are and stand for. Our understanding of eschatology should ask us, if we have "run with the footmen" and they have wearied us, then how "canst thou contend with horses?" (Jer. 12:5).

In short, what our understanding of prophecy and the final events should tell us is that real courage comes, not from going with what's popular, but from going with what's true, even if it means being mocked, derided, and classed with "flat-earthers and bigots."

-⌒-

The Principle of Prophecy

After Isaac Newton proved that the universe worked by mathematically precise laws, many physicists in the nineteenth century believed that once these laws were understood, scientists would be able to predict everything that would happen in the universe.

By the beginning of the twentieth century, however, Max Planck and

Werner Heisenberg (who developed quantum mechanics) argued that scientists were unable even to *measure* the universe precisely, much less predict future events. "It is very difficult," said quantum mechanic Neils Bohr, "to make an accurate prediction, especially about the future."

That's a lesson that Seventh-day Adventists have been slow to learn. Around the turn of the twentieth century, for example, Adventist Bible students studying the prophecies of Daniel and Revelation made numerous predictions about Turkey that in every case turned out wrong. In the 1930s and 1940s Adventists predicted that the Jews would never return to Palestine. In the *Watchman* (December 1936) Roy Frann Cottrell wrote: "But careful study of both the Old and New Testaments reveals that the Hebrew race will never again be reestablished in the Holy Land." (Just so I don't sound too judgmental, a few years ago yours truly predicted that Pat Robertson would run for president in 1992.)

Though I've learned my lesson, others haven't. The church is constantly inundated with predictions about final events and the dates they're to occur. Times have been set through the seventies, eighties, and into the nineties for everything from the return of Christ to the time of trouble to even a giant asteroid that was supposed to kill one third of the earth's population in 1994.

(Interestingly enough, the year that the asteroid was supposed to hit the earth, Jupiter got pelted instead. Right event, wrong planet!)

The difficult time sequences of Daniel, particularly chapters 11 and 12, have been fertile ground for calculating dates of the Sunday law, the Second Coming, and the unleashing of the seven seals.

Yet all these predictions—no matter who makes them or how they come to their conclusions—have one thing in common: they've always turned out wrong.

Many of these problems could be avoided if we would follow a principle that Jesus Himself established regarding the essential purpose of prophecy. "Now I tell you before it come, that, when it is come to pass, ye may believe that I am he" (John 13:19).

Jesus showed that prophecy isn't so much to enable us to predict events; prophecy rather is given to strengthen our faith after the events have happened. In other words, prophecy becomes more meaningful *after* it has been fulfilled, because we can then *look back* and see that the events we've been told about have indeed "come to pass."

For instance, the faith-building aspect of Daniel 2 isn't the promise of

God's final kingdom, which hasn't come yet; the faith-building comes rather from the prophecies that have already been fulfilled centuries after Daniel wrote. By looking back and seeing the history of the world unfold as predicted, we are strengthened to trust in the things that, though predicted, have not yet come to pass, such as the establishment of the final kingdom in the sequence of kingdoms in Daniel 2.

In contrast, when dates are set for future events—such as the time when this final kingdom will be established—and the predicted time passes without the event taking place (as they inevitably have done) faith is weakened, not strengthened.

Of course, the three angels' messages deal with prophecies such as the mark of the beast, and we need to understand what these symbols mean. But speculating about the prophetic fulfillment, particularly dates, is always risky. That's why you don't need to be a quantum physicist to know that when it comes to prophecy, we must not lean too heavily on what we think will happen, but on what already has.

---◦◦◦---

The Primacy of the Prophecy

After walking to a creek one summer morning for a short devotion, I opened my Hebrew Bible to Daniel 8 and 15 minutes later left with a radical new appreciation of verse 14, the cleansing of the sanctuary.

To begin, Daniel 8 consists of two sections—a vision (verses 1-14) and then an explanation of the vision (verses 15-27).

The vision itself consists of four major components. Daniel first sees "a ram which had two horns" (verse 3); then he sees a "he goat [that] came from the west on the face of the whole earth" (verse 5); next "a little horn, which waxed exceeding great, toward the south, and toward the east, and toward the pleasant land" (verse 9); and finally the vision ends with verse 14, the cleansing of the sanctuary: "And he said unto me, Unto two thousand and three hundred days; then shall the sanctuary be cleansed."

The first 14 verses of the chapter (the vision) depict four prime elements: a ram, a goat, a little horn, and the cleansing of the sanctuary.

The rest of the chapter, verses 15-27, explains these elements in the order in which they appear. "The ram which thou sawest having two horns are the kings of Media and Persia" (verse 20). The prophecy names the first component: Media-Persia. "And the rough goat is the king of Grecia" (verse 21). The prophecy names the second as well: Greece. Verses 23-26 then describe the third element, the little horn, depicting it as a powerful persecuting entity that not only attacks God's people but even stands up "against the Prince of princes" (verse 25). Though Media-Persia is depicted as "great" (verse 4) and Greece as "very great" (verse 8), the little horn power coming up after Greece is described as "exceeding great" (verse 9). One doesn't have to be a historian to know that the kingdom that came up immediately after Greece—a kingdom greater than Greece or Media-Persia—a persecuting power that ultimately will be "broken without hand" (verse 25), is only Rome, both pagan and papal (in the Bible Rome is depicted as one power). Finally, the explanation ends by discussing the fourth and final element in the vision: that of the 2300-day prophecy, but doesn't explain it.

Thus the four major elements in Daniel 8 are:

1. Media-Persia
2. Greece
3. Pagan/papal Rome
4. Cleansing of the sanctuary

Now, the first element, Media-Persia, certainly played an important role in the history of the world and of God's people (Media-Persia freed the Jews from Babylonian captivity and paved the way for them to reestablish the Hebrew nation). Greece too, particularly under the exploits of Alexander the Great, impacted the world and God's church in a big way. The third element, Rome, of course played a major role in the world and with God's people, and will do so until the Second Coming.

The crucial point: if only four elements exist in the chapter and the first three are so significant, what does that automatically say about the fourth (the cleansing of the sanctuary), except that it must be of major significance as well? Because the first three elements play pivotal roles in history, the fourth and climactic one must be pivotal too.

Thus whatever one believes Daniel 8:14 means, the cleansing of the sanctuary at the end of the 2300 days must be a crucial event on par with, and even exceeding, the great powers that preceded it in the vision. Even if one rejects the Adventist interpretation—that of the pre-Advent judgment, which leads to the Second Coming (see Dan. 7:9-11, 22, 26)—the context of the prophecy proves that the cleansing of the sanctuary must be of prime importance.

Interestingly enough, no other denomination does much with the text except to relegate it to localized events in Jerusalem about 150 years before Christ. Adventists alone emphasize Daniel 8:14, and considering the importance the chapter itself gives to the text, we're right on track in doing so.

∽

Sure Bet

The day I could pass for 18, I completed what had become a rite of passage for those of us who sprouted into adulthood among the less-than-hallowed streets of Miami Beach—I went to place a few bucks on a greyhound at the Biscayne Dog Track. As I walked through the turnstile and entered the complex, however, I immediately saw the 12 ticket windows—10 that took your money and two that gave out winnings. Now, I'm no statistician (even if I am the son of one), but I knew that five-to-one odds against you aren't a good bet. From that moment I realized that the dog track could be only a losing venture.

About seven years later I read Daniel 2 for the first time in my life. And just as I saw that the odds worked against me at the track, I saw that the fulfillment of the prophecy that predicts Christ will establish His eternal kingdom presented odds that only a fool could bet against.

Think about Daniel 2 purely from the odds alone.

Babylon, "the head of gold" (verse 38),* came and went, just as Daniel had predicted.

That's one for one.

The second kingdom, Media-Persia ("And in your place another kingdom will arise, earthier than you" [verse 39]), came and went, as predicted.

That's two for two.

The third kingdom, Greece ("And a third kingdom, another, of brass, which will rule over all the earth" [verse 39]), came and went, again as predicted.

Three out of three.

The fourth kingdom, pagan Rome ("And the fourth kingdom will be strong as iron" [verse 40]), rose and fell, again according to the prophecy.

That's four out of four.

Next Daniel said that this fourth kingdom—unlike the others, which were each replaced by another single empire—would be broken up into lesser kingdoms, some stronger than others, and that these kingdoms would never be united, even through the bonds of family and marriage. "And that you saw the feet and the toes, partly clay, partly iron, the kingdom shall be divided . . . and as the toes of the feet were partly iron and partly clay, the kingdom will be partly strong and partly broken. And as you saw the iron mixed with the clay, they shall mingle themselves with men's seed, but they will not cleave one to another, even as iron will not mix with clay" (verses 41-43). What better—and more accurate—prediction could have been made about the breakup of the pagan Roman Empire into what ultimately has become the divided nations (some weak, some strong) of modern, intermarried Europe?

That's five for five.

What's left? Only God establishing His eternal kingdom. "And in the days of those kings will the God of heaven set up an everlasting kingdom that will not be destroyed" (verse 44).

Look at the odds. Babylon, Media-Persia, Greece, pagan Rome, modern Europe—all came in order, just as Daniel had predicted (notice too that the Lord has here given us something as concrete, irrefutable, and accessible as world history upon which to help establish our faith). The only thing left in the prophecy, and the only thing that we, from our perspective, haven't yet seen fulfilled, is the last one, Christ's eternal kingdom.

Thus what the Lord presents in this chapter are tremendous odds that the promise of His coming and the establishment of His kingdom will be fulfilled. Daniel was right on the first five. Why bet against him on the last?

As I said, I'm not a statistician, but my dad is, and when I called him for this column, he said that anyone betting with those odds in their favor had an excellent chance of winning (as opposed to the racetrack odds). From pure statistics alone, then, we have every reason to believe the Bible promise of Christ's return. The math works clearly and overtly in our favor. Meanwhile, those who reject the Bible predictions about Christ's return are gambling with odds heavily *against* them.

They have a better chance of winning at the dog track.

---

* All Aramaic translations are mine.

98

Solely, Totally, and Only Rome

T ime to revise our worn, outdated views of papal Rome, which are rooted in nineteenth-century American prejudice, not in sound prophetic principles? Time to rethink our antipathy to the papal system, which has greatly changed since Vatican Council II? Time to decide whether we are one Christian church among many, or whether—by clinging to our antiquated prophetic views—we "must stand alone over and against all other Christian bodies"?

Not only have these questions been asked recently, some people have answered *Yes* to them all. I reject not just the answers but the questions, too.

First, the Seventh-day Adventist understanding of papal Rome is founded not on nineteenth-century American bigotry, but on the prophecies of Daniel interpreted through the historicist method, the method that the texts themselves demand. The chronological sequence of Babylon, Media-Persia, Greece, and Rome (of which three are mentioned by name) proves that the prophecies unveil a successive progression of world *history,* which is why the *historicist* interpretation had been used by Jewish and Christian scholars centuries before Adventists adopted it.

In the statue of Daniel 2 itself, Babylon (gold), Media-Persia (silver), and Greece (bronze) are all followed by the iron in the legs that extends through the toes to the end of time. What power comes up after Greece and, though eventually changing form (the iron mixes with clay in the feet and toes), remains the same power until supernaturally destroyed? It's Rome—solely, totally, and only Rome, which rises after Greece and ends only when the world does (remember, even though mixed with clay in the feet and toes, the *iron* goes from Greece all the way to the end, proving that the power after Greece is the last earthly one).

In Daniel 7, after Babylon (lion), Media-Persia (bear), and Greece (leopard), a fourth beast appears, one that comes up after Greece and extends to the end of time when supernaturally destroyed, just like the iron in Daniel 2 (the little horn power that arises in the head of the fourth beast is still part of the fourth beast). What power comes after Greece and remains (in another form) until the end?

Solely, totally, and only Rome.

In Daniel 8, after Media-Persia and Greece (which are named!), another power arises and remains until destroyed "without hand" (verse 25). What power comes after Greece and endures until the end?

Again—solely, totally, and only Rome. And because Scripture often depicts pagan and papal Rome as *one power,* and because the pagan phase has long disappeared, papal Rome alone remains, the entity unmistakably depicted—and condemned—in Scripture.

The premise, therefore, that Adventist attitudes toward Rome arose, not from correct biblical hermeneutics, but from prejudice is like claiming that Western aversion to pedophilia is rooted, not in moral absolutes, but in hatred of ancient Athens.

And what about the claims that Rome has changed? The new *Catechism of the Catholic Church* proves that Rome is no more in harmony with the gospel now than when, at the Council of Trent, it damned to hell those who believed in justification by faith alone. Rome *can't* change, at least not in what matters, because Scripture clearly depicts its prophetic role, and God is never wrong. Does this mean that those in Rome are predestined to their fate? No, it means only that the Lord, with His perfect foreknowledge, saw what these people—using their free will—would ultimately do, and He warned us about it in His Word.

And the last point, that our position on Rome somehow pits us against "all other churches." Even if one accepted that dubious assertion, my answer would be *So what?* Sure, we shouldn't be putting up incendiary billboards; but we shouldn't water down present truth, either. We have been called to preach the three angels' messages of Revelation 14, which includes a distinct cry against "the beast." We can't do that without implicating "the beast." If, in this age of ecumenism, that's offensive to some, let it be offensive.

When we compromise on Rome (an entity that began through compromise), we become like what we have condemned. Thus, when we compromise on Rome, we condemn ourselves.

Debunking "The Context Problem"

A dventists have long taught that the judgment in Daniel 7 (verses 10, 22, 26) is a parallel depiction, but from a different perspective, of the cleansing of the sanctuary in Daniel 8:14. A comparison of chapters 7 and 8 proves our position correct.

Opponents, however, claim that in both chapters the focus is on the little-horn power, and that the verses have nothing to do with the saints or a judgment of the saints. Critics call it "the context problem," and they claim it destroys the Adventist understanding of the judgment.

How do we respond?

First, look closely at the question, in Daniel 8:13, that brings the answer in verse 14. It reads, "How long *shall be* the vision concerning the daily *sacrifice,* and the transgression of desolation, to give both the sanctuary and the host to be trodden under foot?"

The words italicized in the text aren't in the Hebrew; the translators placed them there to clarify (they hoped) the meaning of the text. Notice the word "concerning." It's not in the original text, and with good reason, because Hebrew grammar forbids its being there.

Thus the question isn't about just the activity of the little horn. It's about everything depicted in the chapter: the vision about the ram and the goat (Media-Persia and Greece) and the little horn (pagan and papal Rome). A literal translation would read, "How long the vision, the daily, and the transgression of desolation to give the sanctuary and the host a trampling?" In other words, the question lists everything in the vision: Media-Persia, Greece, and Rome. It's not about the activity of the little horn alone.

Nevertheless, the judgment scene in Daniel 7 and the cleansing of the sanctuary in Daniel 8 do occur in the immediate context of the persecuting little horn. Far, however, from debunking our position on the judgment, this reality only enhances it.

How? The answer exists in the Hebrew concept of justice and judgment, which involves the vindication of the innocent *and* the punishment of the guilty. The little horn does evil against God's people; ultimately, there is a judgment that not only vindicates the Lord's people—"and a judgment was made in favor of the saints" (Dan. 7:22, NKJV)—but brings the wicked to final justice ("but the judgment shall sit, and they [the saints] shall take away his dominion, to consume and destroy it unto the end" [verse 26]). In other words, in the context of the pre-Advent judgment (which is the work of Christ in our behalf in the heavenly judgment), the demise of the little horn, the symbol of evil, makes perfect sense.

Here's biblical justice—and it contains both the punishment of the guilty and the vindication of the righteous. "If there be a controversy between men, and they come unto judgment, that the judges may judge them; then they shall justify the righteous, and condemn the wicked" (Deut. 25:1). "Then hear in heaven, and act, and judge Your servants, condemning the wicked, bringing his way on his head, and justifying the righteous by giving him according to his righteousness" (1 Kings 8:32, NKJV). In Daniel 7 judgment is given in favor of the saints in the judgment, a judgment that leads to the final demise of the anti-Christian little horn. In Daniel 8 the cleansing of the sanctuary—an act of vindication for God's people—is shown in the context of little-horn power. And that's because as a result of that cleansing, the little horn power is "broken without hand" (Dan. 8:25), that is, the little horn is supernaturally destroyed. Saints vindicated, evil punished. That's biblical!

The question in verse 13 could be paraphrased like this: *How long will all these things, from the rise of Media-Persia, to the rise of Greece, and finally to Rome's attack on Christ's heavenly ministry, be allowed to go on?*

The answer, to paraphrase Daniel 8:14, is that these things will continue for 2,300 more years, but then the final judgment will begin, the sanctuary in heaven will be cleansed, the persecuting little-horn power will be destroyed, and the saints—vindicated in the judgment—will receive the eternal kingdom.

Sure, there's a context problem in Daniel 7 and 8: those who reject the pre-Advent judgment on the argument presented above don't understand the context of God's judgment, that's all.

—◦∾◦—

Nonsense Multiplied

In my 24 years as an Adventist, I never cease to be amazed by arguments used *within the church* by those who—under the guise of modifying our theology—undermine it instead.

I'm thinking of "the apotelesmatic principle," the notion that prophecy can have two or more fulfillments. While that idea itself isn't problematic, how it's used is, because the one place these folks apply it—the prophecies of Daniel 2, 7, 8—is one place in Scripture that utterly refutes it.

What justification exists, for instance, in the claim that Daniel 2 can have multiple fulfillment when Daniel says the prophecy is about four great kingdoms that will arise until God's final kingdom is established (Dan. 2:37-44)? He doesn't say that these metals mean one thing in one era, another thing in another, and something else in another. Daniel says, without obfuscation, what the prophecy covers: a series of world empires that climax at the Second Coming.

The case against multiple fulfillments is stronger when Daniel 2, 7, and 8 are looked at together. These chapters deal with five kingdoms, four earthly and one divine:

Babylon (Dan. 2:38)

Media-Persia (Dan. 8:20)

Greece (Dan. 8:21)

(Unnamed fourth kingdom)

God's eternal kingdom (Dan. 2:44; 7:14, 18, 27).

Some make a big deal out of the fact that the fourth kingdom is not specifically named in Daniel. But what major power, arising after Greece, extends down to the time of the end? The answer, of course, is Rome.

In fact, though Daniel himself doesn't specifically name Rome, the New Testament does (Luke 2:1; John 11:48; Matt. 22:17; Luke 3:1; Acts 25:21). Jesus, talking about the future destruction of Jerusalem, said: "And when ye shall see Jerusalem compassed with armies, then know that the desolation thereof is nigh. Then let them which are in Judaea flee to the mountains; and let them which are in the midst of it depart out; and let not them that are in the countries enter there into" (Luke 21:20, 21). In the parallel passage in Matthew Jesus says, "When ye therefore shall see the abomination of desolation, spoken of by Daniel the prophet, stand in the holy place, (whoso readeth, let him understand:) Then let them which be in Judaea flee into the mountains" (Matt. 24:15, 16).

Thus, in the context of the destruction of Jerusalem, *by the Romans* (one would be hard-pressed to find a serious scholar who doesn't believe that Jesus isn't referring here to the Roman destruction of Jerusalem in A.D. 70), Jesus linked the Roman Empire to the book of Daniel. Jesus, therefore, not only points to Rome, but places it within Daniel itself, where three times phrasing linked to "the abomination of desolation" spoken of by Jesus, in reference to Daniel, is found (Dan. 9:27; 11:31; 12:11). Of particular interest, too, is its use in Daniel 9:24-27, a prophecy that most scholars see pointing to, among other things, the destruction of Jerusalem by Rome, a prophecy that is tied directly to both Daniel 7 and Daniel 8. And seeing that, historically, Rome arose after Greece, its identification as the fourth power is a no-brainer.

The point is this: Daniel doesn't come right out and name Rome because the New Testament does it for us. Thus, following the Protestant formula of the Bible being its own interpreter, all five empires in Daniel are named in the Bible.

Therefore, with all five elements in Daniel 2, 7, and 8 identified, what justification exists for the notion that these powers can have various fulfillments in different times through earth's history? As I wrote in my book *Graffiti in the Holy of Holies* (Pacific Press, 2003): "Considering what's named, massive empires immovably and immutably rooted in world history itself, the idea that we can somehow give these prophecies different fulfillments in different eras certainly doesn't arise from anything inherent in the texts themselves." On the contrary, everything in the texts themselves denies the idea of multiple fulfillments, at least here in Daniel.

Thus the "apotelesmatic principle" remains what it has always been, a figment of scholarly imagination inapplicable in the one place some among us apply it.

The Sabbath
and the End

A lifelong Adventist recently sat in my office at the General Conference and said that he rejected the church's end-time scenario. Even if a Sunday law was passed, he insisted, he still wouldn't believe.

"Ellen White wrote for her time," he asserted. "She's not relevant today."

His words revealed two fallacies, one intellectual, one experiential.

To begin, who says the Adventist concept of the end is based on Ellen White? She has added a lot, no doubt, but you don't need her—indeed, you shouldn't need her—to believe our basic eschatological scenario.

After all, it's Daniel 7, not Ellen White, that tells of a persecuting historical power that thought "to change times and laws" (verse 25), a power that reappears in Revelation, again in the context of persecution.

Next Revelation, not Ellen White—using language lifted from the Sabbath commandment, one of the laws that this power "changed"—calls for God's faithful to "worship him that made heaven, and earth, and the sea, and the fountains of waters" (Rev. 14:7), in contrast to those who "worship the beast" and his image. (Interestingly enough, the language about worshipping "the image" comes from Daniel 3, where the religious freedom issue centered on the other commandment changed by this power, the prohibition against idol worship). Finally, in the midst of the warning about false worship, the faithful are described in Revelation as those who "keep the commandments of God" (Rev. 14:12), which by necessity include the Sabbath, the only commandment that points directly to the Creator of the "heaven, and earth, and the sea, and the fountains of waters."

Believe whatever you want, but you don't need Ellen White to see that the Sabbath will play a key role in the end.

The man's words, however, revealed an even deeper problem—an experiential one.

What Sabbathkeeper, when Friday envelops everything in Sabbath shadows, hasn't at some point experienced just how basic and primal Sabbath is? In a manner so powerful that—without the possibility of exception—it consumes 24 hours a week of our lives, the Sabbath confronts us with the realization that our life, breath, and existence come only from that Creator. Only by our experiencing the magnitude of what Sabbath contains can the day point us to what it means. By keeping Sabbath, we outwardly manifest belief that God is our Creator and Redeemer, and that all we have, are, or ever could be depends upon Him. Only after having experienced the Sabbath in all its sweeping power and grasping what it symbolizes about God's authority can we truly comprehend the momentous issues at stake regarding its observance.

The Sabbath isn't simply about resting 24 hours a week; it's about God's sovereignty. The final controversy isn't about a day; it's about whom we worship and serve. Time, in and of itself, means nothing. God could have blessed and sanctified the first, third, or fifth day. The change of the Sabbath deals instead with God's sovereignty. By usurping prerogatives that belong only to God, the power that brought that change usurps God Himself. If the seventh-day Sabbath is the outward sign of God's sovereignty, the first-day replacement that sweeps away that day sweeps away that sovereignty as well, or at least attempts to.

When we experience in the Sabbath the reality of God as Creator and Redeemer, and then realize that all this truth about God—which is contained in the Sabbath only because He placed it there—was usurped by a human institution (the same one that reappears in the book of Revelation), we can only shudder at the arrogance, audacity, and apostasy involved. Only then will the real issue regarding the final events—and the role of the Sabbath in them—be fully comprehended.

Of course, questions, even hard ones, remain. But it's the nature of epistemology that black holes exist in everything we know, even in what we know for sure. Fortunately, in the crucial area of last-day events and the Second Coming we haven't been left to flounder. Instead, through the "sure word of prophecy" (2 Peter 1:19), we have more than enough reason to trust in the truths that have been poured out upon us for the past century, truths that—as my friend's words revealed—need to touch both the head and the heart to really take root in the soul.

~

The Mark
of the Beast

When I first joined the Adventist Church, every Bible study I gave was on the mark of the beast. Everyone I met, even casually, I had to warn about the mark of the beast. I even used to write graffiti on walls about the mark of the beast. (One time I scribbled on a bathroom wall something about Sunay and the mark of the beast, only to find the next day that someone had written underneath it, "No way—Cliff!").

Since the 1800s Seventh-day Adventists have taught that the three angels' messages of Revelation 14 are "present truth," God's last cry of mercy to a fallen world before the second coming of Christ. Though the foundation of this message is the "everlasting gospel" (Rev. 14:6), it includes this warning: "If any man worship the beast and his image, and receive his mark in his forehead, or in his hand, the same shall drink of the wine of the wrath of God"(verses 9, 10).

To be faithful to our gospel commission, then, we must teach about the mark of the beast, which means that the change of the Sabbath will arise—and that, of course, implicates Rome.

The challenge, particularly for the church, is how to present this delicate issue in a manner sensitive to the great cultural, religious, and social transformations of the past century and yet remain true to Scripture.

This question became especially pertinent early last fall, when various newspapers picked up an Associated Press report about a book published by the Review and Herald Publishing Association. The report said that the book, *God's Answers to Your Questions* (a customized *Bible Readings for the Home*) "likens the papacy to the beast in the book of Revelation, an ally of Satan in the world's final days." It then quoted the book: "Those who acknowledge the supremacy of the beast by yielding obedience to the law of God as changed and enforced by the papacy. . . worship the beast. . . . Such will take the side of Satan in his rebellion against God's authority."

Not exactly the best way to win friends and influence enemies, especially as Catholics and Protestants have been putting aside religious differences so they can cooperate politically (an interesting development in the light of Adventist eschatology).

In such an environment, how do we spread our message? As Christ did, of course.

Why did Jesus immediately tell the Samaritan woman at the well that He was the Messiah when, in contrast, He didn't do the same with the Jews? Because the woman was ready for it; the Jews weren't. Jesus used tact, sensitivity, and care in His outreach in order to offend as few as possible.

That's our example. Sooner or later the message will offend someone (something's wrong if it doesn't), and even Jesus, tactful and sensitive as He was, crossed those who didn't want to hear what He had to say. Nevertheless, just as Jesus—always sensitive to the environment in which He was ministering—tailored His words in response to that environment, we need to do likewise.

Indeed, the harsh polemic of a century ago won't fly in the present environment of political and religious correctness. If in her day, when hatred between Catholics and Protestants in America wasn't much better than what exists in Northern Ireland now, Ellen White could tell the church to deal tactfully with this issue, how much more applicable are those words now, when leading Catholics and Protestant in the United States recently signed a document (*Evangelicals and Catholics Together*) calling for both groups to put aside doctrinal difference and strive for unity in Christ (another interesting development in the light of Adventist eschatology)?

No question, we have a Bible-based message (more relevant all the time) that must never be diluted or compromised, no matter how potentially offensive. But what we must do is present this message as Jesus did, in a manner sensitive to the environment in which it's being preached.

Because after all, whatever you write (and wherever you write it, even on a bathroom wall), you can never be sure what will follow.

An Apocalyptic Twist

Martin Luther once called the pope "the head of the accursed church of all the worst scoundrels on earth," "a vicar of the devil," "an adversary of Christ," the "antichrist," and "the man of sin."

However strong the language, his words reflected the universal conviction among early Reformers that Rome was the antichrist.

Thus Protestant evangelist Jack Van Impe's new video—which warns that "Satan's end-time global ruler, the Antichrist, and his associate, the false prophet," will "arise out of a revived Roman Empire"—sounds like what Protestants have been saying for centuries.

But not quite. Unlike his predecessors, who usually named the pope as antichrist, Van Impe uses the pope to "expose" the antichrist instead! In *Startling Revelations: Pope John Paul II,* this Protestant warns that "apostates" in the Roman Catholic Church, staunch opponents of John Paul's "conservatism on doctrine and morals," could be the antichrist power itself; and according to Van Impe, the pope exposes them as such.

"Protestants," writes Van Impe, "have literally been flabbergasted to know that the pope is right on target concerning this final end-time event."

Startling Revelations begins with Van Impe affirming just how orthodox "classical Catholics" are in their doctrinal beliefs, and how much they have in common with traditional Protestants on points such as the deity of Christ, the virgin birth, atonement through Christ's death, and the Second Coming—in contrast to "liberals" in both traditions who deny these beliefs.

Then, quoting extensively from devout Catholic Malachi Martin—who warns about liberalism in the Roman Church—Van Impe says that these trends are part of the apostasy and false teachings that Scripture warns will precede the Second Coming. In other words, Van Impe basically melds Roman Catholicism with Protestantism and then decries the humanist, New Age, and higher critical teachings in the Roman Church just as much as if it were in his own Protestant one.

To buttress his newfangled premise, Van Impe quotes Bible verses that he believes predicted this apostasy in Catholicism. He warns, for example, that the actions of unfaithful bishops and other prelates were fulfillments of John's warning: "Little children, it is the last time: and as ye have heard that antichrist shall come, even now are there many antichrists; whereby we know that it is the last time: They went out from us, but they were not of us" (1 John 2:18, 19). The idea being that though these apostates from Romanism were once Christian, because of their deviation from church doctrine they were no longer so. Says Van Impe: "They went out from us."

This man actually views these trends in the Roman Church as a fulfillment of Paul's warning: "Let no man deceive you by any means: for that day shall not come, except there come a falling away first, and that man of sin be revealed, the son of perdition" (2 Thess. 2:3)—a verse that Protestants have for centuries applied to Rome and the pope himself!

Of course, Adventists have long expected that the major divisions between Catholics and Protestants would be healed, at least enough for both groups to fulfill their prophetic roles as outlined in Revelation 13 and 14. Though we haven't been given dates or much detail about how it will all come to pass, the trends—everything from a papal encyclical last year calling for the unity of all Christians by the year 2000 to a document in which some Catholics and Evangelicals affirmed their oneness in Christ as a springboard for political activism—certainly seem to affirm our interpretation.

Nevertheless, it was still incredible to listen to a conservative Protestant minister stress the doctrinal unity between "classical Catholics" and Protestants, and then warn that deviation from Roman Catholic doctrine by Roman Catholics is a sign of end-time apostasy.

Van Impe doesn't have it quite right. The sign of the end isn't what the video's about; the sign *is* the video itself!

Mr. Wojtyla's
Sabbath Day

One afternoon this summer little got done in the General Conference, because people (at least in the offices I visited) were busy devouring the apostolic letter by Pope John Paul II, *Dies Domini*—a lengthy, detailed, and passionate plea by the pontiff for Roman Catholics to keep Sunday holy.

Of course, the hype (in ways so utterly Adventist) immediately started. Within a week of the document's release I was in Norway, where rumor was that the pope had warned in the letter that those who didn't conform to Sunday worship would have to be "dealt with." Maybe the pope did write that somewhere, but it wasn't in my copy of *Dies Domini*.

My copy did, though, have passing references to "laws concerning Sunday rest," which would "enable everyone to keep the Lord's Day holy." It also talked about an encyclical by John Paul's predecessor Leo XIII, which stressed "Sunday rest as a worker's right which the State must guarantee." John Paul also wrote that "in the particular circumstances of our own time, Christians will naturally strive to ensure that civil legislation respects their duty to keep Sunday holy."

He's right: civil legislation should respect their duty to keep Sunday, just as it should respect ours to keep Sabbath. How that is accomplished is,

no doubt, another matter (one fraught with apocalyptic consequences)—
but in the end the pope didn't say anything particularly new or extraordinary regarding Sunday laws. One doesn't need *Dies Domini* to know that
he favors them.

The fascinating aspect of the letter, however, wasn't politics, but theology. Mr. Wojtyla wasted lots of ink trying to justify theologically the
change of the Sabbath from Saturday to Sunday. Page after page attempts
to "recover the deep doctrinal foundations underlying the church's pre-
cept, so that the abiding value of Sunday in the Christian life will be clear
to all the faithful."

What's clear, however, is that however effective the quotes are that we
love to use—in which priests and other Roman Catholic officials brag
about how the Catholic Church changed the Sabbath day to Sunday—that
position doesn't seem to be the official one.

Instead the pope goes to great pains, using the same retreaded arguments, to prove that the seventh-day Sabbath "foretells the sacred day of
the new and final covenant." In fostering this argument, however, Mr.
Wojtyla is reduced to quoting Saint Jerome, Saint Gregory, and Saint Basil,
getting them to say what Saint Peter, Saint Paul, and Saint John don't. The
pope even resorts to the Creation story, and—pulling language directly
from the Sabbath texts—tries fruitlessly to buttress the position that
"Sunday is the day of rest because it is the day 'blessed' by God and 'made
holy' by Him, set apart from the other days to be, among all of them, 'the
Lord's Day.'"

The attempt to find in Sunday a fulfillment of the Sabbath has, in fact,
largely been abandoned (for lack of evidence) by many Evangelical scholars, who argue instead that "Sunday is a new day of worship that was chosen to commemorate the unique salvation-historical event of the death and
resurrection of Christ, rather than merely being another day for celebrat-
ing the Sabbath" (*From Sabbath to Lord's Day*, Zondervan), another theological excursion doomed to shipwreck upon the shoals of Scripture.

What can account, then, for the pope's lengthy attempt to justify
Sunday from the Bible?

My guess is that Seventh-day Adventists—with our solid, Bible-based
defense of the Sabbath—have made an impact, that our arguments have,
indeed, had an influence wherever we have preached and taught them.
After all, how could they not? The pope had to try to deal with them directly because we have been dealing with them powerfully and effectively

for more than a century and a half. He couldn't ignore us or our arguments any longer.

However, with all due respect, *Dies Domini* is the latest proof that even the "vicar of Christ" can't get from the Bible what simply isn't there.

～

The Reasonable Observer

From the moment I joined the Seventh-day Adventist Church I faced those within the system who expressed not only disbelief of, but nauseous contempt for, our prophetic interpretations. Having been given my first Bible study on America in prophecy during John Paul II's 1979 triumphal visit to the United States, I have never understood the blindness of those who insisted that our "traditional" interpretation of last-day events was outdated, outmoded, and simply wrong, even after the pope had been paraded around "Protestant" America like a football hero. John 9, in which the Pharisees, despite Christ's healing of the boy blind from birth—could nevertheless declare, "This man is not of God," became so relevant. Rather than make history, we (I saw) repeat it.

Of course, I joined the church almost 20 years ago, when the Soviet Union's massive military might covered the globe, when Protestants were still "protesting" something, when no one of stature talked about "civil legislation" to protect Sunday, and when Pat Robertson was nothing but a TV preacher healing hemorrhoids over the airwaves.

There is in law a phrase known as "the reasonable observer," a fictitious personage who supposedly could look at a situation and without prejudice come to a reasonable conclusion regarding it. I have often wondered: What would this "reasonable observer"—looking at what Adventists have said would happen and at what is indeed happening—conclude about our unique eschatology?

More than a century ago we had been predicting that Catholics and Protestants—with a 400-year history of animosity that often led to violence—would eventually unite, at least on common points. In the past few years influential Protestants and Catholics in America have signed documents such as *Evangelicals and Catholics Together* and *The Gift of Salvation,* which stress that both communions have so much in common that they are really "one in Christ."

We also predicted that the United States would enforce the mark of the beast on the world. Not too long ago the U.S. wasn't even able to kick Fidel Castro out of Cuba because of Soviet military might. Now, however, the Soviet Union has disappeared and the United States, the world's only superpower, is certainly poised to fulfill its prophetic role.

For years I've listened to some Adventists mock the notion that the Sabbath/Sunday controversy could be relevant in a secular, modern world. This idea, they said, was just Ellen White writing for her time, not ours. I wonder what they're saying now, since Pope John Paul II's pastoral letter encouraged not only Sunday worship but "civil legislation" to help it along. Though the pope's letter doesn't mean that blue laws are imminent, it does mean—beyond question—that the Sabbath/Sunday controversy, far from being some antiquated nineteenth-century North American notion, is now a late-twentieth-century issue of worldwide concern (apparently the pope doesn't read left-wing Adventist literature).

And finally, these people mocked the idea of the Christian church ever assuming in America the kind of political control outlined in Ellen White's book *The Great Controversy*. Today the Christian Right, epitomized by Pat Robertson's Christian Coalition—deemed the most "powerful grassroots political movement in America"—has massive power over one of the nation's two dominant political parties and will be a major player in the next millennium.

So what do we have? A United States as the unrivaled world power. The pope urging Sunday worship. Catholics and Protestants uniting theologically. And conservative Catholics and Protestants working in America to gain political control.

Though many issues remain unanswered, I still ask, What would a "reasonable observer"—looking at what we have said would happen and what is happening—have to conclude?

First, such a person would have to conclude that Seventh-day Adventists have incredibly good reasons to continue trusting in the prophetic scenario they have taught and preached about for more than 100 years. Second, the observer would have to conclude that though modern versions of the John 9 Pharisees continue among us, we should smile when they scoff, pat them gently on the head, say something like "God bless you," and move on, trusting in the great prophetic truths

113

our God has graciously poured out upon us in abundance. It's the only reasonable thing to do.

—∞—

The Hole Behind Dunkin' Donuts

L ast Friday, in a cemetery north of Philadelphia, off Route 1, across from a Radisson, around the corner from a Texaco station and be- hind a Dunkin' Donuts—we buried my best friend from the Miami Beach days. He was 43 years old. Breast cancer.

As I stood there looking at the quiet casket (traffic from Route 1 ir- reverently loud in the background), I thought about all that George Zifferblatt and I had done together as teenagers: the boating, the spearfish- ing, the lobsterpoaching, the wild boar hunting (I know, a wild boar hunter doesn't quite fit my nerdy image). And now for all these things *(and so much more)* to climax, to converge, and to end at a single point, a hole in the ground behind a Dunkin' Donuts? It makes no sense.

Yet because so much of the world *does* make sense, irrevocably so, in that it's logical, rational, purposeful (the sun gives us light and heat, plants make air, gravity holds us to the earth, the heart pumps blood), it's the height of absurdity for human life (the beneficiary of all these sensible, logical, and purposeful natural phenomena) to end in such meaninglessness. How can so many of the individual and finite things of nature—in and of themselves re- plete with points and opulent with purpose—so beautifully, precisely, and artfully climax into nothing more than a hole behind Dunkin' Donuts?

They can't; or at least they're not supposed to. Which is why standing there I was struck again by just how fundamental the Second Coming is. Without it and the hope it contains (the resurrection of our bodies into an immortal sinless existence) all that we have believed, lived for, and pro- mulgated as Seventh-day Adventists crumbles into the dust of lies.

The Second Coming isn't the epilogue, the appendix, or the afterword of the sad story that we all find ourselves written into as tragic characters who always die off; the Second Coming is, instead, the raison d'être of all the pages, all the scenes, all the dialogues and transitions and chapters and sentences and commas and periods that precede it. Without it, the story never ends but just goes on and on, one miserable scene after another, like a long and trashy novel. Apart from the hope that Christ's return offers, life is, as Shakespeare wrote, "a tale told by an idiot, full of sound and fury, signifying nothing."

I find it fascinating too that the Second Coming and the resurrection of the dead that attends it are not truths that one can learn from natural law. They are a priori to nothing. These are not promises that inductive reasoning can derive from axioms (and they certainly aren't axioms themselves). The stars at night don't herald in letters of fire the promise of eternal life. The waves don't hint at promises of resurrection. The birds chirping outside our bedroom windows don't express this truth (and, in fact, without it they would be singing our dirges). Nothing in nature, history, or logic portends or even hints at it. On the contrary, in and of themselves, nature and history tell us that when we die we turn into nothing but carbon and dust; the closest we'll come to life again is when we fertilize a tree or feed the bacteria that dissolve our corpses.

Instead, I know about the Second Coming only because I've been told about it. I believe what I've been told about the Second Coming because I believe what I've been told about the First. "Now if Christ be preached that he rose from the dead, how say some among you that there is no resurrection of the dead?" (1 Cor. 15:12). The surety of Jesus' second advent rests with the surety of His first; His resurrection contains the promise of ours. Without the Second Coming, the first was an empty gesture, an exercise in futility. Only the Second Coming validates the cross; without His return, Christ hung there in vain.

Thus as sure as we are that Christ died for our sins at the First Advent is as sure as we can be that He will resurrect us to life at the Second. Otherwise all that we believe in, teach about, and hope for will end in nothing, at least nothing more than a hole behind Dunkin' Donuts.

~

The September 11 Sky

I am writing these words two tortuous weeks after the Twin Towers attack: rubble in Manhattan still smolders, rumors of war wrinkle the air, and American flags are as ubiquitous here as the visage of Saddam Hussein is in Iraq.

I do see hints, however, of normalcy: people don't stare in wonder and fear at every jetliner that soars overhead, newspaper headlines can no longer be read from 40 feet away, and the radio actually has commercials again. And, on a more personal note, I no longer feel as if everything I do is meaningless.

Distanced timewise from the catastrophe, with the numbness fading like Novocain two hours after a pulled tooth, I want to share some thoughts (take them or leave them), and the gist of those thoughts is this: I've never before been so grateful for my Adventist faith as I am now.

First, because of Jesus, because of what He accomplished at the cross, even if I were in one of those planes or buildings (my office was not more than a morning commute from the Pentagon), death would seem like an instant of darkness followed by the infinite light of eternity with Christ. Faith, an intelligent, reasoned faith in who Christ is and what He offers us because of what He has done for us—it's worth more than anything the world can give, a truth that I especially cherish now.

Next, as I watched the two towers collapse (I had my whole family there in June), these texts stomped through my head: "Love not the world, neither the things that are in the world. . . . For all that is in the world, the lust of the flesh, and the lust of the eyes, and the pride of life . . . is of the world. And the world passeth away, and the lust thereof: but he that doeth the will of God abideth for ever" (1 John 2:15-17). How desperate that flesh and lust must be, that is, to love a world so inimical, so harsh and un-forgiving to both; and to love *the things* of the world, things that coddle that flesh and tickle that lust before curdling and then killing them both.

People want permanence, people want stability, people want order, but they cling to a world that offers only the sound of time passing through matter (or is that matter passing through time?). Either way, what's left when the sounds end? Lives lived for the sake of life itself? Please! That's like plucking wings off flies. If the World Trade Center towers can't stand, what in the world can? That's why, more than ever, I'm so thankful my hope isn't in this world or the things of it, for they pass away so quickly, so easily, and in ways unimaginable.

Finally, since becoming an Adventist, I have always believed that the United States could never fulfill its prophetic role without major changes. *Major* changes. In the few days following the atrocity, we saw how quickly change, major change, can come. The issue isn't whether these changes will lead to prophetic fulfillment (I'm not going down that road, because

I have no idea where these acts of terrorism will lead). All I'm saying is that for the lamblike beast to speak as a dragon, the beast will have to change, and these attacks—if they prove nothing else prophetically—prove how quickly the beast can, indeed, change (imagine if the death toll were 10 times higher!). One thing for sure, our prophetic scenario seems easier to envision after September 11, 2001, than before it.

What can I say, other than that I'm just so thankful for what the Lord has given me through the truths entrusted to this church. I'm thankful, not just for the framework to understand why such evil happens (the great controversy scenario), or even for the more specific framework regarding last-day events (America in prophecy and all that). What I am most thankful for is the hope of the Second Coming, a hope guaranteed by the First (after all, what good was the First without the Second?)—a hope that nothing can take away, not even death and terror raining down from the September 11 sky.

Between the Strokes, Again

Near the beginning of the past century, an Adventist Church leader, writing about end-time events, said something to the effect of "When I say that the Turk will do this, he does that; when I say that the Turk will do that, he does this. I am determined never to say another word about the Turk."

Considering the fate of "The Turk," at least in the context of end-time events, his was a wise decision. The confession reveals, too, the risks of interpreting current events through the paradigm of Bible prophecy. Scripture paints last-day events with broad strokes. Ellen White, painting those same events, uses strokes that—if not as wide as Scripture's—are still wide enough. Once we start prognosticating between those strokes, we need to be cautious. Trust me, I've learned the hard way.

Recently, though, I read something that's got me between the strokes, again. I found it in *Cigar Aficionado* magazine. Now, before some saint chokes on a Veja-Link, I don't read *Cigar Aficionado*. Instead, after hearing about it, I—wanting the original for this column (instead of some bowdlerized Internet version)—coughed up five bucks for the issue (can you see me turning *that* receipt in to the treasury?).

The Mules That Angels Ride

In *Cigar Aficionado* (vol. 12, no. 1) General Tommy Franks, who led American forces against Saddam in 2003, warned that in the event of a major terrorist attack, we could lose the "freedom and liberty" that we have had for more than 200 years. "It means," the general said, "the potential of a weapon of mass destruction and a terrorist, massive casualty-producing event somewhere in the Western world—it may be in the United States of America—that causes our population to question our own Constitution and to begin to militarize our country in order to avoid a repeat of another mass-casualty-producing event. Which, in fact, then begins to potentially unravel the fabric of our Constitution."

Wow! What struck me hardest about this quote was that since September 11 the grand high-muck-a-mucks inside the Beltway never talk about *if* there's going to be another attack, but only about *when*. Let's be honest: considering world events, who really thinks we're not going to get it in the keister again?

Remember the fear, the helplessness, even desperation, of September 11? Imagine, though, something biological, chemical—*nuclear*? If a crude "dirty bomb" in the back of a van in Brooklyn released radiation for five square blocks, regardless of the "low" casualties the psychological effect would be devastating. Who, meanwhile, can fathom the radical changes—in our psyche, self-understanding, and national priorities—were half of Los Angeles incinerated along with a few *hundred thousand* people? And with no visible enemy to retaliate against, which would mean we would have no assurance that something worse wouldn't follow, Americans would be desperate to protect themselves, no matter what.

In such circumstances the stars on Old Glory could become fists, its stripes bars of iron—and most Americans wouldn't care. If letting U.S. attorney General John Ashcroft read my e-mail, tap my phone, and peek in my bedroom window would save my family from getting nuked by al-Qaeda, let him. Most people, I imagine, would agree—which explains General Franks' fear about "the fabric of our Constitution."

Inspiration tells us that the lamblike beast of Revelation 13 will speak like a dragon; it doesn't tell us how or why. From my earliest days as an Adventist I always believed that only something drastic would cause the United States to repudiate the Constitution and fulfill its prophetic destiny. What that would be, I don't know, but a weapon-of-mass-destruction attack could easily do the trick. Who, amid a smallpox scourge infecting millions, is going to get worked up over selective incorporation, due process, and the Fourteenth Amendment?

Sooner or later the big party that's America will be over. Precisely how, who knows? ("The Turk," in whatever form, has proved elusive.) This ignorance should cause us not only to tread cautiously, especially when between the strokes, but to focus mostly upon the One who promised to be with us, "even unto the end of the world" (Matt. 28:20), regardless of what ushers it in.

Jerusalem and Athens

IN THE BEGINNING, all the great scientific thinkers, the giants—Descartes, Galileo, Copernicus, Newton, et al—worked on the presupposition of God's existence. They saw their research as simply revealing the handiwork of God in creation. How things have changed. Between Isaac Newton's words "O God! I think thy thoughts after Thee!" and Stephen Hawking's (who occupies the same chair at Cambridge that Newton did), "The human race is just a chemical scum on a moderate-sized planet, orbiting around a very average star in the outer suburb of one among hundreds of billions of galaxies," a whole dimension, unable to fit in test tubes or conform to formulas, has been written out of nature and moved to the realm of myth. The church, our church even, has not been immune to the powerful consequences of this radical shift in worldviews. In this section, I look at some of the challenges science as now practiced presents to faith, and then do my best to work through them, in hopes that some answers I've found might be helpful to others as well.

Jerusalem and Athens

T hough I always feel somewhat uncomfortable when introduced as a speaker, this introduction (at a camp meeting years ago) should be emblazoned in bronze.

"Now, we have Clifford Goldstein here," the host emoted into the mike, "and he's a 100-percent full-blooded Jew!" Though he meant well, I felt like a cow at an auction ("We have a 100-percent full-blooded Holstein here"). Perhaps, after reaching the podium, I should have let them inspect my teeth.

Nevertheless, he was right: I'm a 100-percent full-blooded Jew. At least in genetic descent and religious roots. However, in my head I'm Greek. I love the Greek philosophers' attempt to discover truth through reason, empiricism, and logical speculation. Never mind that they got much of it wrong; it was the way that they tried to pry truth from the stars, from the rocks, and from raw, unencumbered logic that I find fascinating.

However, a recent head-on collision with a thought has radically re-aligned my epistemological prejudices. Think about it: Of all the truths that we can ever know, what's the most important? Of course, that Jesus Christ at the cross bore the penalty of all our sins so that we never have to bear them ourselves, and that through faith in Him we can stand perfect before God in judgment because we are clothed in His righteousness (not our own), the only means of attaining eternal life. In contrast to this truth, questions about whether philosophers should be kings, or whether Achilles can catch up to the tortoise, or whether you can step in the same river twice become banal and trite.

Yet (and here's the punch line) how did I learn this most important truth about Christ and the cross? Through science? Logic? Empirical anal-

121

ysis? Mathematics? No way! I know it only because *I have been told it,* spoon-fed it through revelatory drips and dribbles from God's Word.

Science, logic, and math might lead to profound truths about everything from the Excluded Middle to the elusive nature of light, but none of these disciplines—no matter how exhaustively pursued—terminates at the cross. At God, or gods? Perhaps. At a Creator, or even an intelligent Designer? Maybe. But to Jesus Christ, the incarnate Son of God, who sacrificed Himself for the sins of the world? Never. You might as well use a Geiger counter to interpret dreams.

Now, if science, empiricism, reason, in and of themselves, can never teach me the most important thing that I need to know, salvation in Jesus Christ, why should I allow things such as science, logic, and empiricism to define my understanding of that salvation? Because these disciplines, even at their best, could never lead me to Jesus, it makes no sense to set them up as the final judge and arbiter of what I believe about Him (Why use pigeon feathers to judge stealth bomber wings?). If none of these disciplines could ever get us to the cross, what makes them the supreme arbiter of what we believe once we're there?

No one is denying the utility of these disciplines; it's the role that they've assumed in the area of faith that I question. For too many people, even professed Christians, the Word of God—rather than being the standard by which they judge and critique the conclusions of science, or reason, or empiricism—is, instead, judged and critiqued by these disciplines. What jives with science, logic, empiricism (or at least whatever the latest versions happen to be), that's what we keep; what clashes, that's what we dismiss.

"In vain do they worship me," said Jesus, "teaching as doctrines the precepts of men. You leave the commandment of God, and hold fast the tradition of men" (Mark 7:7, RSV). Science, logic, and empiricism are nothing but modern renditions of the precepts and traditions of humanity, now garbed in the robes of modernity. And though precepts and traditions can be fine—even true—they're *not* the Word of God, and they certainly don't provide the supreme standard for judging it.

No question, truth has come out of Athens. But Truth itself came from Jerusalem, Truth too important to be left for us to try to figure out on our own. That's why it had to be told us. Do we listen, or do we filter it through the very tools that have proved inadequate to teach us that Truth in the first place?

Phenomenon and Noumenon

Somewhere amid her inspired tomes Ellen White wrote of a biblical figure whose first child gave him new revelations about God. In my case, it wasn't my first child who did that for me—it was my dog, a pug named Fergie.

I had not owned a dog before, and when my wife brought the squat beast home 11 years ago, I soon realized that Fergie was a sentient being who confronted much of the same reality I did—even if it came funneled to her through sensors different from, and often keener than, mine. After all, Fergie could hear, smell, and (residing closer to terra firma) see things that I couldn't. And so I've wondered, *Whose view of reality is more accurate, mine or the mutt's?*

The question isn't frivolous. The implications in it have haunted philosophers and theologians for millennia. Because the world comes to us mediated only through our senses, what's the difference between how the world appears to us and how it really is?

Suppose that instead of two eyes, we had 20, of which five could see in the infrared spectrum, five could see telescopically, and five microscopically. Suppose our ears could pick up the heartbeat of birds, or our noses the waft of bumblebees. Imagine how different reality would appear. Would these different sense perceptions give us a better view of what's out there, or merely a different one just as subjective as what we have now?

German philosopher Immanuel Kant distinguished between the *phenomenon,* the world as it appears, and the *noumenon,* the world as it really is, the world that exists behind our senses. The haunting question is What's the difference between the two?

Writing against the notion that "man is the measure of all things," Plato said that if all it took to know truth were sensations, then a "pig or a dog-faced baboon" could also "be the measure of all things." Reality can't be limited to how it appears because, first, reality comes to us through sensation, and different sensations give us different concepts of reality (such as the difference between mine and Fergie's); and second, so much reality exists beyond our sensations that to limit truth to what we perceive is like limiting "music" to only Hootie and the Blowfish.

Years ago I used an example with my kids (try explaining phenomenon and noumenon to a 5-year-old and a 7-year-old). As we sat in a room, I asked if they heard anything besides our own voices. They said no. I then turned on a radio and ran the dial across the stations. At once music, laughter, and talking filled the room. Those sounds, I said, didn't originate in the box. Instead, they were there, with us, all the time—but, given how we're wired, given the limited peripherals plugged into our brains, given our limited hardware and software, we couldn't detect those radio waves even though they were just as real as the sound of my voice or the light from the window that lifted the room out of darkness and into our view.

There's the world of experience, that which hovers within the squeeze of our senses; and there's the thing-in-itself (the *Ding an sich,* as the Germans call it), which our senses never really grasp but more or less ricochet off, leaving us only murky reflections.

The gap between the phenomenon and the noumenon has helped me better accept, by faith, the reality of the great controversy, a literal battle between supernatural entities just as real as the incessant waves of cellular phone calls moving around us at this moment but out of the reach of our senses. Angels, demons, the Holy Spirit, they're all part of the noumenon, the world as it really is; all we can directly sense is the phenomena, a limited slice of the noumenon itself.

We do, indeed, see "through a glass, darkly" (1 Cor. 13:12), even if the Lord has gingerly sprinkled that glass with shards of light. Scripture does lift what Ellen White calls "the veil which separates the visible from the invisible world" (*Testimonies,* vol. 5, p. 467); yet much remains curtained—for both me and my dog.

Unlike Fergie, however, I have the promise that one day the veil will be removed, and "then shall I know even as also I am known" (1 Cor. 13:12).

The SF

A dear saint—apparently liking my column in which I talked about buying a $35 book I couldn't afford (Mar. 28, 2002)—sent me $35 to buy more. After wrestling with my conscience over keeping the money (my conscience lost, handily), I bought two books: one with poetry by Rilke and Paul Hoffman's *The Man Who Loved Only Numbers: The Story of Paul Erdös and the Search for Mathematical Truth*. Though I'd much prefer writing about Rilke (trust me, it's coming), these words are about Erdös instead.

Probably the greatest mathematician of the twentieth century, Paul Erdös (1913-1996) was so eccentric that he made Einstein look normal. He was 11 before he ever tied his shoes, 21 before he ever buttered toast, and died without ever boiling an egg.

Erdös lived on the road, traveling from math conference to math conference, owning nothing but math notebooks and a suitcase or two. His life consisted of math, nothing else. A typical letter from him would read something like this: "I am in Australia. Tomorrow I leave for Hungary. Let k be the largest integer . . ." A mathematician named Mike Plummer told about a Christmas Eve pounding on his door. He opened it and there stood Erdös, who said, "Plummer, Merry Christmas. Let f of n be the following function . . ."

From amid his labyrinthine whirring and computations, Paul Erdös often talked about "the SF," "the Supreme Fascist"—his name for God. Which got me thinking: what a perfect example of the limits of natural theology.

From the time of Pythagoras (pre-Christ) even to today, some mathematicians have expressed a mystical, almost religious devotion to numbers. ("God," said Plato, "always geometrizes.") Encountering incredible beauty, coherence, and complexity in mathematics, many believe that numbers exist in some sort of eternal, unchanging realm that mathematicians—with awe, fascination, and hard work—occasionally stumble into. "Mathematical reality," wrote Alain Connes, "possesses a consistency truly superior to that of sensory intuition, an unexplained coherence that is independent of our reasoning system."

The famous Mandelbrot set, for instance, a fractal, is an incredibly complex and stunningly beautiful geometric form created when one does some simple repetitive operation on a graph with the equation $Z = Z^2 + C$, with Z being a complex number and C being a certain fixed number. The images are awesome. "The Mandelbrot set," wrote Oxford mathematician Roger Penrose, "is not an invention of the human mind: it was a discovery. Like Mount Everest, the Mandelbrot set is just there!"

Meanwhile, the Pythagorean theorem (the square of the hypotenuse of a right-angle triangle is equal to the sum of the squares of the other two sides), and pi (the ratio of the circumference of a circle to its diameter), and phi (the Golden Mean, a ratio that is present in various growth patterns) are just a few mathematical realities that, while hardly proving the existence of God, certainly could imply it. Even Erdös, when discovering a proof he liked, would say, "It was straight from the book."

Whose book? The Supreme Fascist's, who else's? And that's the point. Whatever Erdös and these others believe they have learned about God from mathematics, it's never enough to teach them about His true nature and character. They get, at best, only glimpses of His power, creativity, and genius; but nothing in their equations, axioms, or proofs reveals His self-sacrificing love, a love that led Him to pay—in Himself, through His Son—the penalty for our sins in order that we can have eternal life. To know about that, we need special revelation, which we have been given in His Word—and nowhere else.

How crucial, then, that we never allow ourselves as a church, or as individuals, to be swept away, or even slightly moved, by the higher critical currents that inevitably will weaken our trust in the Bible. For the Bible alone shows us that the God we serve isn't the SF, the Supreme Fascist, but the one who valued our freedom so much that He suffered in our stead the penalty for our abuse of that freedom—a truth that higher math, even the highest math, can never reveal.

Because it's not written in numbers. It's written in blood.

⌘

The Title of This Column Is False

R ead the title of this column: "The Title of This Column Is False." Now, if what the title says about itself is true, then the title is (as it says) false. What a paradox. The title is true only if it is false. On the other hand, if "The Title of This Column is False" is false—then it must be true, because if it is false that it's false, then it's true. Thus another paradox: Only if the title is false can it be true.

Take a second example, found in (of all places) the Bible. In Titus 1:12, the apostle Paul wrote, "One of themselves, even a prophet of their own, said, The Cretians are always liars." Now, it's a Cretian prophet who says that "Cretians are always liars." But if Cretians are always liars, then that must include the Cretian who said that Cretians are always liars, and the statement by someone who is always a liar must also be a lie. The statement, then, that Cretians always are liars must be a lie; therefore, Cretians are not always liars—which means that the only way the statement (by a Cretian) that "Cretians are always liars" could be true is if the words "Cretians are always liars" is false.

Welcome—that is, to the mind-twisting world of self-referential statements, statements that talk about themselves, like the one you are reading now and that is about to end before you get to the period that is coming up fast but not before the this sentence ends.

Cool, huh?

Different types of self-referential statements exist, some paradoxical, some not. Try the following. "This sentence contains exactly threee erors." But, you say it contains only two errors. Right—and that's its third one. Or this one, known as Berry's paradox (named after the librarian who created it). It refers to "the least integer not nameable in fewer than 19 syllables"—yet the line just named that integer in only 18 syllables (count them)! In his *Metamagical Themas* cognitive scientist Douglas Hofstadter gave a real whopper of self-referential confusion with the following. "This sentence does in fact not have the property it claims not to have."

Got it?

Ignore this sentence (indeed, ignore this entire paragraph, but especially the part within the parentheses).

Self-referential statements, however, aren't just gimmicks; on the contrary, they reveal a fundamental limitation of human knowledge, which is that whatever our system of thought, there are certain inherent contradictions impossible to resolve within the system itself. Using the notion of a paradoxical self-referential statement like the one found in the title of this column, Austrian metamathametican Kurt Gödel created his famous incompleteness theorem in which he showed that even within mathematics itself certain inherent contradictions exist that can't be resolved within that system. Logic and reason, inevitably, always break down at a certain point. Or, to put it another way, whatever we know, either secular or sacred, we have to take it (at least to a degree) on faith.

Of course, as Adventists we shouldn't find the limits of logic and reason surprising. We understand belief in what we cannot "prove." In fact, I find it humiliating that of all the things I can know, the most important truth of all—i.e., that Jesus Christ died for all sinners and that by faith we can have eternal life (John 3:16; Rom. 5:8)—is a truth that *I have to be told*. The most crucial aspect of all possible knowledge is one that we can't figure out on our own; logic, reason, empiricism, and science wouldn't get us there. Instead, this, the greatest and most important of all truth, has to be spoon-fed us—a situation that, like self-referential paradoxes, says a lot about the limits of logic and reason when it comes to knowing what really matters.

One slight problem, though. In this column I've been using logic and reason to show the limits of logic and reason, which means that the more effectively I use logic and reason to make my point about the limits of logic and reason, the more effectively I weaken my argument against the limits of logic and reason. Like a self-referential paradox, this column undermines the point it makes by proving it.

Which is only logical.

Got it?

~

Science Fiction

In his famous *History of Science* (1929), Sir William Cecil Dampier wrote, "Science, we have now come to understand, cannot deal with ultimate reality; it can only draw a picture of nature as seen by the human mind."

Shhh . . . this is the best kept secret of the twentieth century, in which science has become to us what Marduk was to the Babylonians and Lenin to the Communists—a god.

Today the ultimate arbiter of truth, the final determiner of knowledge, isn't found in the Bible, but in the lab. "What science cannot tell us," wrote Bertrand Russell, "mankind cannot know." In other words, if it can't be proved scientifically, if it isn't within the realm of empirical inquiry, then it can't be known; instead, it can be only believed (as one might believe that red is prettier than green). Because science, for example, asserts that the dead can't be raised—then they can't (though, actually, Tulane physicist Frank J. Tiler wrote a bizarre book, *The Physics of Immortality,* in which he tried to prove through *physics alone* that the dead will be resurrected).

The deification of science is a great myth of the modern era, akin to deification of the Caesars in an earlier one. Science has its role, no doubt, and works well within it. But just because chlorine's good for killing germs, that doesn't mean you want it for mouthwash. To modify and paraphrase Galileo: science might be able to tell us how the heavens go—but not how we go to heaven.

Indeed, the most important thing we need to know—salvation by faith in Christ—is beyond science. What can the lab teach us about atonement, sin, salvation, redemption, the Second Coming? After all, when science states that we're here only because some conglomeration of inorganic elements turned by chance into a primitive life form that over billions of years evolved into everyone from Sophocles to Cal Ripken, the limits of science become painfully obvious. (Another of my favorites is how the dinosaurs became extinct: supposedly, a giant comet hit the earth and covered it in smoke, killing all the vegetation and thus taking all the brontosauruses, pterodactyls, and so forth with them.)

Not only the limits but the dangers of science (when out of its element) are revealed in a new book, *God, the Evidence,* in which Patrick Glynn attempts to use near-death experiences as proof of immortal human souls. Glynn asserts that modern scientific research "proves" that the experiences of people "leaving" their bodies at "death" and talking to dead relatives are some sort of journey into the "next life."

No wonder Ellen White spent so much time warning about spiritualism in the final deceptions that will sweep the world before the Second Coming. The conscious immortal soul now has the twentieth century's imprimatur of science to back it up—and only fundamentalist Bible hicks argue against it.

The church isn't immune either. Some Bible teachers claim to use the "scientific approach" to study Scripture, as if that method will reveal the true meaning of the text. Again, what can science—which denies a literal six-day creation and a universal flood—tell us about Jesus giving sight to the man blind from birth, the feeding of the 5,000, the raising of Lazarus, or the healing of Jairus' daughter? It can't tell us anything, except that these events could not have happened. These teachers would be better off using the "voodoo approach" for interpreting the text (at least voodoo has room for faith).

Fyodor Dostoyevsky, in *The Brothers Karamazov* (1880), expressed concern, through the character Father Paissy, about the danger of attributing too much to science: "Remember," the monk said, "that the science of this world, which has become great, has, especially in the last century, analyzed everything divine handed down to us in the holy books. After this cruel analysis the learned of this world have nothing left of all that was sacred of old. But they have analyzed only the parts and overlooked the whole, and indeed their blindness is marvellous. Yet the whole still stands steadfast before their eyes, and the gates of hell shall not prevail against it."

Good counsel all the way around.

⁓

Quashed by Culture

An atheist in Italy scribbled these words on a wall: "There is no God—and Mary is his mother."

However ridiculous, this graffiti unearths something primal about humanity: we're hopelessly autochthonic. Whatever our ism, we view, interpret, and express it through the icons, axioms, and presuppositions of our culture, our soil, our birth. We can no more escape these filters than we can our thought, because it's through these filters that we think.

The Christian church is hardly immune to this phenomenon, either—ours included. What else explains why (for instance) La Sierra University is in California, and Southern Adventist University is in Tennessee? It couldn't have been any other way.

The results are palpable, perhaps best expressed by poet Ann Sexton, who—in her quest for God—wrote: "She prayed in all the churches of the world/and learned a great deal about culture."

How sad. Ann comes to church, seeking God, and learns about . . . what? Michael Jackson?

The church's greatest failure has been its inability to mesh within a culture without allowing that culture to bowdlerize, or even neutralize, the teachings that make Christianity true. Take the most consequential example: How long after the cross did culture turn the church of Christ into antichrist? Not long at all.

Another example of this failure, and the subsequent consequences, occurred in sixteenth and seventeenth centuries, when Christianity was confronted with the new cosmology of Kepler, Copernicus, and Galileo. Though often depicted as an example of the church refusing progress, this struggle is better explained as what happens when the church allows itself to be dominated by the icons, philosophies, and culture of its time.

Christianity was, at that time, dominated by an Aristotelian world-view, basically a pagan cosmology that—mostly through the work of Thomas Aquinas (with a little help from Dante)—had become incorporated into Christian thought. This idea of a stationary, immovable earth surrounded by a hierarchy of celestial entities, all moving around it in various cycles and epicycles, wasn't biblical, wasn't based on a sound exegesis of the Bible. It was, instead, Greek philosophy as expounded by Aristotle (who believed, among other things, that the planets needed anywhere from 49 to 55 gods to keep them moving). Yet this system of thought became the mode by which the church, kissing up (par usual) to the latest cultural trends, interpreted the world—and Scripture. As historian Richard Tarns expressed it: "But with the church's gradual acceptance of that work [of Thomas Aquinas], the Aristotelian corpus was elevated to the status of Christian dogma."

And, lest we think this was just a Catholic thing, Luther derided Copernicus as "an upstart astrologer" and—along with such other Reformers as Calvin and Melanchthon—wanted to suppress the pernicious heresy that the earth moved.

Today, of course, the cultural norm isn't the pagan Roman pantheon, or Aristotelianism; instead, the prevailing zeitgeist is science, the Queen of Heaven with a test tube. It's kind of ironic: science, which began essentially as a revolt against all authority, has now become that authority, the ultimate standard through which all belief, including Christianity, must be judged.

The late Michael Polanyi, philosopher of science and professor of physical chemistry at the University of Manchester, argued that the "ideal goals of science are nonsensical" because, he writes, science functions on the assumption that all existence can be explained "in terms of forces acting between atomic particles."

That approach might work, and only partially, with biology and chemistry, but to evaluate Christianity in those terms? Please! It's like using an MRI to evaluate poetry. Yet science and the "scientific method" have become the cultural icons of our era, and the Christian church is proving itself no less immune to them than our predecessors were to Baal, the Roman sun god, and Aristotelianism. Tragically, in the same way that culture quashed truth back then, it's doing the same today as well. The results are no less problematic, either.

Take poor Ann Sexton. Maybe, when coming to church, if she had found Christ instead of culture, she might have died a born-again Christian instead of suicide.

⟨∾⟩

The Myths of a "Progressive Faith"

According to a front-page bleep in the Washington *Post,* scientists have just determined the order of all 34 million chemical "letters" that spell out the genetic code for "a single human chromosome."

Now, maybe my neural paths are hopelessly overgrown with tendrils of biblical creationism, but something about 34 million chemical letters on a *single* human chromosome (not to mention the 1.6 billion letters on all 46 chromosomes—*per cell!*) speaks to me, not about science, or even about genetics—but about mythology.

Nobody, of course, *believes* (as in present tense) in myths. The ancient Egyptians didn't build massive pyramids because of myths about life after death; the Incas didn't tear out their children's hearts for myths about angry gods; and millions today haven't rejected biblical creation for myths about natural selection, macroevolution, and survival of the fittest. Myths are not what we believe; they are, instead, what becomes of truths we *no longer* believe (truth, on the other hand, is what remains even after we stop believing it).

Reports about 34 million pieces of information on a *single* human chromosome (and others like it) make me wonder, How soon until evolution is demoted—as were Quetzalcoatl, the Egyptian underworld, and Zeus—to myth? When physicist Roger Penrose, hardly a biblical creationist, said that the chance of an ordered universe like ours happening at random is 10 to the 10 to the thirtieth power *against* (a number far larger than the number of atomic *particles* believed to exist in the known universe), it's obvious that the Romans had more logical reasons to believe in the birth of Minerva from the brains of Jupiter than our contemporaries do in the birth of humanity from Darwin's mutations and natural selections.

What tale, for example, do evolutionists tell about the human heart, which pumps life-giving blood to the body's 120 trillion cells? Remember, the heart can't work for more than a few minutes without blood being pumped to it. When the blood stops, so does the heart (it's what's known as a heart attack), right? So how did the heart survive all those long, cold

132

millions of years before blood—an almost infinitely complex substance filled with billions of cells, each cell containing (among myriad other mind-boggling details) 1.6 billion genetic letters—finally evolved into something that could keep the heart alive in order to pump blood to itself?

Not only can the heart not exist without blood, but blood can't exist without the heart, because the heart pumps blood to the bones, which make red blood cells, and red blood cells feed the heart the oxygen it needs to survive. (What fantastic myth explains how blood first got to the oxygen in the lungs without being first pumped there by the heart, which couldn't pump blood without first having oxygen?) The question is How did the bones exist all those millions of years before finally evolving into a factory for red blood cells—when bones themselves need the red blood cells to exist? *Bones can't exist without the very thing that they themselves manufacture.* One needs a myth more incredible than Minerva's birth to explain how something creates the very thing that it itself first needed to exist. And we have it; it's called evolution.

The incredible thing about myths, however, is the readiness with which people believe them (remember, they're not myths at the time of belief). Even in our church we have those who—in the words of an Adventist college president (*Spectrum,* March 1996, p. 28)—exhibited a "progressive faith" by incorporating evolution into their, ahem, *Adventism.*

Biblical history, however, is replete with the fruits of such "progressive faiths." Ancient Israel "progressed" past Moses and the prophets, right to myths of Baal, Moloch, Greek dualism (immortality of the soul), and, eventually, Roman sun worship (Sunday worship). Those melding the myth of evolution with the faith of Jesus are, in fact, nothing but twentieth-century versions of the ancient Israelites who mixed their children's blood in with their sin offerings to Yahweh.

We all need to believe in something, so why not choose what's true? Some choose evolution as the source of those 34 million bits of information per *chromosome;* some choose Jesus, who—according to God's Word—created humans in a day.

The biggest myth, however, is to think that you can choose both.

~

The Book
of the Cosmos

Fingers clenched around a book I couldn't afford (having just splurged on an armful of editions two weeks earlier), I realigned the text back on the shelf, wandered over to my wife, and sheepishly muttered, "I saw this book, but, ah, like, I don't think I should spend $35 . . . do you?"

"Just get it," she said.

"You convinced me!"

Best $35 I ever borrowed from Visa. The tome's called *The Book of the Cosmos: Imagining the Universe From Heraclitus to Hawking* (Perseus, 2000). Starting with the Genesis creation account and ending with authors still metabolizing protein, editor Dennis Danielson traces the spiritual, scientific, and speculative history of thought regarding the most fundamental of all human questions—How did we get here, and why?

Though the book is exclusively excerpts—from Parmenides to Paul Davies, from Aristotle to Fred Hoyle—Danielson does add his own ideas to the selections, and sometimes (but not always) his words can be quite insightful.

Commenting, for instance, on passages from the book of John (1:1-14) and Colossians (1:13-20), Danielson writes, "Put theologically, the authority and efficacy of Christ as Redeemer are intimately linked to his 'authorship' and agency as Creator." A Seventh-day Adventist couldn't have said it better (in fact, it's better that an Adventist didn't say it).

Fascinating too was a selection from Cicero (106-43 B.C.), who argued against life and reason emerging from something that possessed neither. "If flutes playing tunefully were sprouting on an olive tree," wrote Cicero, "you would surely have no doubt that the olive tree had some knowledge of flute-playing. . . . Why then is the universe not accounted animate and wise, when it brings forth from itself creatures which are animate and wise?"

To put it differently, How could "animate and wise" beings such as ourselves arise in a universe that—if not itself "animate and wise"—at least had a Creator who was?

How exciting to read authors centuries before Copernicus arguing for the motion of the earth, or to read the words that helped get

Giordano Bruno burned at the stake, or to read Galileo's glee at "having discovered four planets, neither known or observed by anyone before my time."

The most revealing section came at the end, with the intellectual gymnastics of those scientists determined to dismiss a Creator (or at least a Designer) despite every indication of one. For instance, according to one excerpt, the chances of our universe forming have been estimated at 10^{229} to 1, a rather large number considering that the number of protons and neutrons (that's protons and neutrons!) in all the visible universe is only 10^{80}. Scientist Martin Rees argued that rather than these incredible odds being evidence for a Creator, there's simply 10^{229} random universes out there, and ours just happens to be one of them.

Responding to Rees's fandangled theory of origins, scientist Lee Smolin wrote, "To argue this way is not to reason; it is simply to give up looking for a rational explanation."

Rees isn't alone in twisting logic in order to squeeze God out of the picture. Though sheer logic teaches that nothing can arise from nothing, don't tell that to scientist Alan Guth, who has argued that "everything can be created out of nothing."

Well, almost nothing. For Mr. Guth, "nothing" turns out to be a false vacuum patch "10^{26} in diameter" and "10^{32} solar masses"—small, but hardly "nothing." And it's out of this "nothing" that, supposedly, all that is—the entire universe (which he calls "the ultimate free lunch")—has arisen. Mocking Guth's cosmology, David Berlinski, also quoted in *The Book of the Cosmos,* wrote that for most people "nothingness, like death, is not a matter that admits of degrees," a point apparently lost on Mr. Guth.

Fortunately it's not all such highbrow, pseudoscientific nincompoopery. Indeed, Danielson ends *The Book of the Cosmos* with an essay by astronomer Owen Gingerich, who in a section titled "Do the Heavens Declare?" writes: "I cannot prove that God exists or that God's claims on our lives are what makes life meaningful. But do the heavens declare the glory of God? I think so. The universe is so full of such wonderful things that I can hardly think otherwise." Amen.

Sometimes it pays to spend money you don't have.

The Quiet Revolution

Whatever their differences, many of the modern era's common-isms—communism, atheism, secularism, positivism, Marxism, whatever—are all premised on one similar notion, which is: we are here by blind chance alone, nothing but "an accidental collation of atoms" that have made us unfortunate by-products of a random, even un-friendly, universe.

Wrote Jacques Monod, "The ancient covenant is in pieces: man at last knows that he is alone in the unfeeling immensity of the universe, out of which he has emerged only by chance."

Well, that's one way to look at it. On the other hand, science in the past few years has undergone what *Time* magazine has called a "quiet rev-olution"—one that at its core undermines the foundation of these isms.

At the heart of this "quiet revolution" is the anthropic principle (from the Greek word *anthropos,* "human being"), which says, essentially, that the universe is so finely and sensitively tuned, so delicate in its basic structural balance, that if any one of a number of crucial variables were off even by an almost infinitesimal percentage, then humanity could not exist.

"The universe," said one scientist, "seems to have evolved with man in mind." In other words, according to the anthropic principle, humanity *(anthropos)* is the *ultimate end and purpose of the whole universe*—a position that goes much further than what biblical creationists believe.

"Far from being some curious sideshow or accident," wrote Patrick Glynn, "humanity, or life at least, appear to be the goal toward which the entire universe has been intricately orchestrated, the logical center around which a whole host of physical values and relations had been exquisitely and precisely arranged."

Physicist-mathematician Paul Davies, in his book *God and the New Physics,* gives one example of just how finely tuned the universe is. Talking about the incredible balance between gravity (which pulls objects toward each other) and the force of the big bang (which pushes objects away from each other), Davies wrote that "had the big bang been weaker, the cosmos would have soon fallen back on itself in a big crunch. On the other hand, had it been stronger, the cosmic material would have dispersed so rapidly that galaxies would not have formed. Either way the structure of the universe seems to depend very sensitively on the precise matching of explo-sive rigor to gravitating power."

How precisely matched? Davies writes that if this balance had been off by 1 to a staggering 10^{60}, we couldn't exist. "To give meaning to these numbers," Davies continues, "suppose you wanted to fire a bullet at a one-inch target on the other side of the observable universe, 20 billion light-years away. Your aim would have to be accurate to that same part in 10^{60}."

This and other "cosmic coincidences"—such as the delicate balance between the strong and weak forces or the balance between the masses of subatomic particles—have forced many scientists to reevaluate their most basic assumptions about the nature of the universe, which is that rather than creation being a random event, it appears to have been a purposely and carefully crafted one.

Of course, science is now only seeing what Isaiah proclaimed thou-sands of years ago: "For thus saith the Lord that created the heavens; God himself that formed the earth and made it; he hath established it, he cre-ated it not in vain, he formed it to be inhabited" (Isa. 45:18).

Unfortunately, what most of these scientists don't know is that every week, for 24 hours, without exception—and maybe even while they sit in their labs and marvel at the creation—God's immutable, indestructible, and eternal sign of that creation passes over them, silently bearing witness to what their research, computations, and calculating are eloquently saying.

Thus, as science is now catching up with theology, we should see more than ever just how relevant, crucial, and fundamental the seventh-day Sabbath (and in fact the whole three angels' messages) really is. Indeed, while the anthropic principle overtly undermines most of the world's com-mon and popular-isms, it quietly and powerfully affirms the one-ism we call our own.

Love and Matter

Squat and pillow-propped on the bed where he was from the softer dust first formed, my son, my firstborn son, sat. A few months old, and swathed in a cotton gown that closed around his unused soles, he looked like a pint-sized sack, only with a head—and a smile glinted in drool. I stood alongside him and, with a fistful of pillow, would bop his bald head; at each blow, with the regularity of natural law, he would let out a spasm of infantile delight.

As I stood, exulting with him in the hilarity of it all, a sudden wave of energy surged out of me and engulfed the child. If dye had been spilled in the air, it would have flowed in the stream that rushed from my flesh and linked me to him with a hold stronger than bone. The room crackled, electric in the love that poured out of me and connected with my little boy.

Now, I wonder: How would an intricate and complicated medical machine interpret this moment of bonding? A flush of dopamine to the frontal lobe? Vasoconstrictors up and down the spine? An endocrine surge? Elevated electrolytes? Perhaps. Yet these physiological manifestations, I'm convinced, could no more explain that moment than optics could Leonardo's *Mona Lisa*.

Voluminous dissertations have no doubt been written on the phrase "So God created man in his own image" (Gen. 1:27)—the points of some contradicting the points of others (even if each terminated in a Ph.D). Whatever, though, the phrase meant, it must at least mean that, as humans, we can love. If "God is love" (1 John 4:8), and we're in the image of God—then my conclusion is (if nothing else) logical.

And here's where all naturalistic, materialistic, and especially evolutionary theories sputter and die. At what point does matter, pure matter, mutate into beings that love? Can carbon and water, or blood and bone even, emerge into fathers who bond with their sons or wives who love their husbands? "Evolution," someone wrote, "is a seamless garment with no holes wherein souls might be imparted from above." Replace "souls" with "love," which must come from above (where else? From electrons and quarks?), and you'll know what I mean.

In a survival-of-the-fittest paradigm, love—which is nothing if not self-sacrifice for another at the expense of self—should have been buried under 20 feet of muck, somewhere between trilobites and Ramapithecus. It's one of those mutations that should have weeded us out, along with the Stegosaurus, eons ago; how, then, did love claw, bite, and scramble to the top of the evolutionary ladder? (It didn't, because there is no ladder.)

Love, instead, represents the highest possible ideal, because when we love we reflect the character of God, who Himself is love. Nothing human is more godlike. That's why, more than being loved, humans need to love. There's a reason that the two most important commandments are commandments to love: through love we are being sanctified and restored into the image of God.

Yet you can't love without pouring something that's essentially you into others, and because others can be fickle, untrustworthy, and fleeting, love leaves you vulnerable. When you love, you give away the most sensitive parts of your soul, a risky venture at best. If for every action there's an opposite and equal reaction, then to the degree that you love is the degree that you suffer.

Which, of course, explains the cross. "For God so loved the world . . ." The degree that God loved is the degree that He suffered. No one knows the pain of love more than God because no one has loved more than God. The great difference between the new earth and this one is, I suppose, that in the new earth love wouldn't come with such costs. Jesus paid them already.

Until then, we love, and suffer for it. But as I picked up my son, my firstborn son, and grasped that giggling bundle against my chest, love was worth it, whatever the cost.

How fortunate that God felt the same way.

⁓

THWACK!

R ead the first sentence of Scripture. Notice, it says nothing about justification, zilch about atonement, and nada about the Second Coming. There are no comments about salvation, redemption, the law, 1888, or even the mark of the beast.

Now, the reason for the omissions is simple, and that's because all these teachings are meaningless psycho-drivel apart from this one: "In the beginning God created the heaven and the earth" (Gen. 1:1).

Aristotle, in his *Metaphysics,* wrote that the only way to understand something is know its *causes.* What brought it into existence? How did it get here? What is its origin?

He's right, and that's why Scripture begins, not with eschatology, soteriology, or Christology, but with causes, in this case the cause being that "God created the heaven and the earth"—the foundation upon which all that follows rests. If you get this cause wrong, everything else will likely be wrong too. This first cause is so crucial that God gave us an in-your-face reminder of it, every week. It's called the Sabbath, and more than point-ing to salvation, redemption, or deliverance, it points to the first cause, cre-ation—because on that, and that alone, all that we believe (such as salvation, redemption, and deliverance) rests. Destroy or weaken this cause, and what follows is destroyed or weakened as well.

No wonder, then, that the Lord has taken one seventh of our lives to help keep the first cause before us, something He didn't do for any other Christian teaching simply because no other Christian teaching has validity apart from this one.

Think about it: most, if not all, of our beliefs as Christians become babble severed from the Creation account. Salvation? The atonement? The cross? What can these mean apart from origins? What is atonement in a world without a Creator? From what are we saved in a godless universe? And if evolution explains us, then the cross is nothing but another mur-dered Jew. How can one make sense of the Fall apart from our origins? What have we fallen from, and to what are we restored? Apart from the biblical account of origins, our most basic beliefs—from the cross to the Second Coming—put us in the same class as flat-earthers, black-helicopter paranoids, and Moonies.

After severing from the denomination to start a new church, a former Adventist minister in Maryland abandoned the fourth commandment. His argument, basically, is that the seventh-day Sabbath is nullified under the new covenant. How amazing that the new covenant nullifies the one spe-cific sign of the only thing that makes the new covenant meaningful: Creation. New covenant, old covenant, the cross, atonement . . . they all become linguistic blabber apart from the first cause, because upon this first cause, and this alone, all these truths (and every other one) rest.

The seventh-day Sabbath is like a nail that—*Thwack!*—with unbroken regularity returns us each week to the foundation of all that we are or could be. We're so busy, running to and fro, spending money, making money, going here, going there, going everywhere, and then—*Thwack!*—Sabbath comes and reattaches us to the ground of our being, the starting point of everything that follows, because everything that's anything to us becomes that only because God created it and us to begin with. The Sabbath doesn't bring us half, a quarter, or nine tenths of the way back; each week—*Thwack!*—it nails us to ground zero, to the most fundamental and elementary level of human existence, the starting point of all that comes after. By returning us to the beginning, the Sabbath gives us a chance each week, in a sense, to "start over," to refocus on who we are, on what's really important, and to remember how we got here and where we ultimately want to go.

With unceasing regularity, and with no exceptions, the Sabbath silently hurls over the horizon and into every crack and cranny of our lives, reminding us that every crack and cranny belongs to our Maker, the One who put us here, the One who "in the beginning" created the heavens and the earth, an act that remains the irrefutable foundation of all Christian belief, and of which the seventh-day Sabbath—*Thwack!*—is the irrefutable, obtrusive, and unyielding sign.

Turtles All
the Way Down

A story (likely apocryphal) is told about philosopher Bertrand Russell, who—having just lectured on the orbit of the earth around the sun—was confronted by a little old woman in tennis shoes who said, "Everyone knows that the earth sits on the back of a giant turtle." Russell, jesting, responded, "What does that turtle sit on, ma'am?" Without missing a beat, she answered, "Another turtle." When he began to ask what that turtle sat on, she cut him short, saying: "Save your breath, sonny. It's turtles all the way down."

Though the butt of the story, the little old woman was, I think, onto something—if not cosmological, then even more fundamental, and that's the nature of human knowledge itself.

Regardless of the difference in beliefs and worldviews, we all work within a system, the framework through which we interpret the world. The system, whatever it is, functions as the lens, the filter, and the template through which we understand reality. The system itself isn't questioned; on the contrary, the system itself provides grist for the questions. The system is to the questions what grammar, logic, and ink are to this sentence.

Of course, every now and then someone steps back and questions the system, which is fine. But upon what premises are the new questions established? New questions presuppose new assumptions, a new starting point beyond, and outside, the old, which is fine. But upon what is that new foundation based? How can you test the system other than by going outside of it, which requires a new foundation, a new system. Again, no problem, assuming that newest foundation is valid. But that can be questioned only by going outside of it, and on and on. . . . *It is turtles all the way down.* Yet we have to stop with something, because sooner or later we have to base our beliefs on something.

"Of course there is justification for belief," wrote philosopher Ludwig Wittgenstein, "but justification comes to an end." And that end always arrives before we reach the ultimate foundation of everything, or what poet Czeslaw Milosz calls "the lining of the world."

Take science, which always works within a system, the framework in which questions are asked and answers are found. Investigation, inquiry, and analysis occur, but only within the system—and only up to a point. Beyond the boundaries of the system, inquiry stops, even though the presuppositions of the system are just that, presuppositions—"truths" accepted as givens though not proved. How can they be, when they form the foundation upon which the questions are asked? Can a scale weigh itself? Thus, even science—for many the "sacral mode of knowledge"—comes with gaps between what's known and what's assumed.

But doesn't Christianity do the same? Of course it does! But Christianity comes with the realization of our epistemological limits built in. It's called faith, and far from being a weakness (as in science), faith is an integral part of that system. It's as if God knew beforehand the limits of human inquiry, and thus built that realization into the system of truth itself, even made it a fundamental component.

Both science and Christianity are, in a sense, groundless, in that both work within frameworks built upon unproven assumptions, things that have to be taken on, well, faith. The big difference is that for Christianity, faith isn't an admission of weakness or failure. On the contrary, faith is an essential part of the package, an a priori acknowledgment that the foundations of knowledge can take us only so far, and then we have to step out beyond the seen or the proven. As the Bible writer said, "Now faith is being sure of what we hope for and certain of what we do not see" (Heb. 11:1, NIV).

However different their approaches, Christianity and science are both faith ventures—systems that, in and of themselves, can't get us to that bottom turtle, even though we know it's there. Whether we're seeking it as tiny superstring loops in 10-dimensional space, or as God Himself, sooner or later faith fills in where our inquiry inevitably, and of necessity, ends.

It's not, then, only the "just" who have to live by faith; scientists do too.

Churchy Things

THIS SECTION CONTAINS, by far, some of my most controversial columns, including the "notorious" "Seventh-day Darwinians," in which I took the radical and wild position that people who are members of our church—especially those who stand in our pulpits and/or teach in our schools—ought, perhaps, to believe our basic teaching, which includes a six literal 24-hour-day creation. *How dare I be so presumptuous?* Maybe some of these columns have been controversial because I have been very forceful in expressing what I believe is Truth (with a capital "T"), a view that many, even among us, find offensive. Why? It's because we live in the postmodern era, when there's no Truth, only lots of little "truths" (your truth and my truth and his truth, those kind of truths); however antithetical (one would think) to our SDA understanding of reality, this world-view has entered the church as well, which could explain some of the antipathy to my bold assertions about us possessing Truth. *That's arrogant, boastful, dogmatic!* So be it! I believe that Truth exists, and that we as a church have been given more of it than any other corporate body in existence now. If that thought, which pervades these columns, is offensive to some among us, let them be offended. They'll get over it.

Limited Options

Imagine you're you living in the times of the first Temple; imagine, too, your disgust at the compromise, worldliness, and accommodation of paganism that had become so rabid the people would sacrifice their children to idols and, later that same day, worship the Lord at the sanctuary (see Eze. 23:39).

Or imagine you're living during the times of the second Temple, and imagine your disgust with the regnant legalism, so icy and extreme that even Jesus had been accused of breaking the law (John 5:16).

In either scenario the question is Where would you go? Back to Egypt and worship Bastet the cat goddess? Or to Babylon and its moon god Sin? Or (in the latter period) maybe you could offer sacrifices to Jupiter. Or join one of the cults that worshipped Caesar. Or if none of these satisfied the longing of your soul, there was always astrology.

But you're you today, not then, even if parallels exist. Depending upon your theological perspective, either the Seventh-day Adventist Church is filled with the same earthliness, compromise, and accommodation that ruined Israel in the first Temple's period, or (from the other side) the Adventist Church is as dogmatic, insular, legalistic, and unprogressive as Israel in the days of Christ.

Aficionados of either perspective, however, face the same question as those who lived in either historical period, which is: Where would you go? If you still want to keep the Sabbath, you wipe out about 99 percent of all your options. If you also wouldn't feel comfortable joining a fellowship that teaches that at death your immortal soul immediately soars into the endless bliss of heaven or descends into the fiery pits of eternal torment, then you've eliminated probably 99.9 percent of the 1 percent of the choices left. Not much remains.

Churchy Things

Maybe that's the way the Lord meant it to be. Maybe truth has always stood out so clearly and distinctly that once people find it and love it, there are few, if any, competitors. I'm not saying that the differences between Adventism and other Protestant faiths are as great as the differences between ancient Judaism and the pagan faiths around it; that would be pushing it. What I am saying, however, is that the differences between Adventism and these churches are still great enough to limit severely the options of someone who, frustrated with the Adventist Church, wants to leave and yet maintain any theological integrity.

Though it was not easy to become a Seventh-day Adventist, now that I'm here it's easy to stay; because as long as I cling to the Sabbath and the nonimmortality of the soul, reality doesn't offer anything close enough to tempt me. If there were all sorts of Sabbathkeeping churches—which taught that death is a sleep until the first or second resurrection—then I might have a problem. But there aren't any, so what's the problem?

Of course, the Adventist Church is an easy target. Whether on the "right" or on the "left" (and even in the "middle"), whether bemoaning the liberalism or the calcified dogmatism within our ranks, people will always find something to complain about, to criticize, and to lambaste (have you been on the Internet lately?). And no doubt in some cases the complaints, the criticism, and the lambasting are deserved.

Nevertheless, the question remains: Where else would you go? Just as truth in the Bible times stood out so clearly in contrast to the error around it, it does today as well. Look around at your options, at what's being taught—eternal torment in hell, the secret rapture, 200 million Chinese invading Israel in the battle of Armageddon, and of course the belief that Jesus changed the Sabbath to Sunday.

I can see the letters coming now: *Goldstein, you're so arrogant. Goldstein, you're so narrow. Goldstein, you're such a denominational jingoist. Blah, blah, blah . . .* (I get so many nasty letters that my frontal lobe has assumed the texture of limestone).

Maybe, I'm all those things and worse; but my character defects aren't the point. The point is this: As long as you believe that the Sabbath and the state of the dead are too important to abandon, you have no real serious options other than the Seventh-day Adventist Church.

Get over it.

And use your influence for good.

Vertical Truths

Many might find it hard to believe I would confess this, but after 20 years as a Seventh-day Adventist (including the past six as an ordained minister) I'm still not comfortable in a church. Even after all these years, when I hear my children (8 and 10) talk about going to "church," I feel a twinge of pain.

It's because of my Jewishness, of course. However secular my background, I was still raised Jewish, and from my earliest years I had always associated Christianity—churches, Jesus, the cross—with oppression, persecution, and anti-Semitism. Jews were Jews, Christians were Christians; they had more weapons that we did, and that was that. The neurons had been formed early on, and it's not so easy to dismantle them now.

In fact, if I could follow my heart, I wouldn't even be a Seventh-day Adventist; I'd be a Messianic Jew instead. Messianics are Jews who have accepted Jesus as the Messiah, but who worship Him as Jews, in synagogues, just as the earliest followers of Jesus did (sorry, folks, but Peter, Paul, James, Barnabas, et al., did not go to church). Messianic Jews know that they don't have to become Gentiles or worship in Gentile traditions in order to follow Jesus. I love Messianic services, Messianic liturgy, and Messianic music (something about singing "Onward, Christian Soldiers!" in a church just doesn't do much for me). In a Messianic synagogue I feel like what I am, a Jew who has accepted his Hebrew Messiah, *Jesuah ben Joseph.*

What's interesting, too, was that an Egyptian Seventh-day Adventist once told me he struggled with the same feelings, only from a Muslim perspective.

Which comes to the crux of why, even despite my heart longings or the sporadic twinges of pain, I'm a Seventh-day Adventist and, through God's grace, will always be one. My feelings, and those of my Egyptian friend, arose from the horizontal, the dimension of the contingent, relative, and constantly changing cultural forms, traditions, and customs that we just happen to be exposed to (if, by fate, I had been raised where my Arab friend was, and he where I was, our roles would be reversed). Though the horizontal has its place, something transcends it, something takes precedence over it, and that's the vertical—the dimension of eternal and unchanging truths, the truths that years ago I sought with all my heart to know no matter the cost to myself, the truths that have made me, not a Muslim, not a Baptist, not even a Messianic Jew, but a Seventh-day Adventist.

Whenever the horizontal conflicts with the vertical, the horizontal has to give, because the horizontal is just fleeting and ephemeral, while the vertical is eternal and transcendent. The horizontal is, essentially, just the world passing away, nothing more; the vertical, in contrast, leads to eternal life, nothing less. If truth were exclusively horizontal, existing in the realm of the human only, there would be no argument: one should do what one feels like doing because there's nothing above to judge whether it's right or wrong. Reality, however, exists in more dimensions than a mere plane.

I love the Messianic worship, the Messianic culture, the Messianic ambiance, but I love "present truth" more, and present truth dictates that I worship in a church that understands the state of the dead (which Messianic Jews don't), a church that understands the eschatological significance of the Sabbath (which Messianic Jews don't), a church (I still cringe at that word, but don't judge me unless you've been in my shoes) that understands Christ's two-phased ministry in the heavenly sanctuary (which Messianic Jews don't). These are vertical truths that transcend culture or tradition, truths that can't be swallowed up and swept away by the emotions, twinges, and biases that the horizontal has etched, hewed, and scribbled into me since birth.

Of course, I'm not narrow enough to believe that one has to be a Seventh-day Adventist to be saved; that's hardly the issue (in fact, that's not the issue at all). But I am narrow enough to want to follow truth, which leaves me no other option than the Seventh-day Adventist Church—even if, as a Jew, I would rather be in a synagogue on Sabbath, worshiping my Messiah *Jesuah HaMaschiah* and chanting, *"Shema Yisrael, Adonai Elohanu, Adonai Echad"* (see Deut. 6:4).

27 Fundamental *Disbeliefs*

To declare that we have 27 fundamental beliefs is to declare that we also have 27 fundamental *disbeliefs*. When we say what we accept, we say what we reject. To assert "what is" is, of logical necessity, to assert "what isn't."

Fundamental belief 1, for instance, states: "The Holy Scriptures, Old and New Testaments, are the written Word of God, given by divine inspiration through holy men of God who spoke and wrote as they were moved by the Holy Spirit." With that affirmation, we automatically reject all higher-critical presuppositions that dismiss Scripture as solely a human production, a mere cultural and historical record (and not a very accurate one, supposedly) of a certain people in a certain time.

Fundamental belief 6 states: "God is Creator of all things. . . . In six days the Lord made 'the heavens and the earth' and all living things upon the earth, and rested on the seventh day of that week." These words implicitly declare what we *don't* believe: the evolutionary model of origins, any a priori materialistic presuppositions about reality that leave out the supernatural, or any worldview that credits our existence to blind, uncaring forces.

Fundamental belief 7 says: "Man and woman were made in the image of God. . . . When our first parents disobeyed God, they denied their dependence upon Him. . . . The image of God in them was marred and they became subject to death. Their descendants share this fallen nature. . . . They are born with weaknesses and tendencies to evil." Again, by stating what we believe, we implicitly state what we don't: namely, all concepts of humanity that proclaim the inherent righteousness of humankind, or which assert that goodness dwells naturally within us.

Fundamental belief 9—By declaring that "in Christ's life of perfect obedience to God's will, His suffering, death, and resurrection, God provided the only means of atonement for human sin," we also declare our belief that any faith, philosophy, or worldview that doesn't accept this understanding of Christ is, quite simply, wrong.

Fundamental belief 23 declares: "There is a sanctuary in heaven, the true tabernacle which the Lord set up and not man. In it Christ ministers on our behalf. . . . In 1844, at the end of the prophetic period of 2300 days, He entered the second and last phase of His atoning ministry." Again, logic necessitates that with these statements we dismiss any claim that denies the existence of the sanctuary in heaven, that denies Christ's ministry there, or that denies the "second and last phase of His atoning ministry," which began in 1844.

The 27 fundamental beliefs are not an attempt to express opinions (such as "We prefer Veja-Links to Grillers"), but facts—and facts, by their very nature, are polemical. Every "fact" denies its negation. To say "The house is red" is to deny that it's blue, green, or yellow. To say that the seventh-day Sabbath is still binding (belief 19) is to reject the position of all who say it isn't.

Perhaps this reality explains the antipathy of some within the church toward the very notion of our openly expressing such fundamental beliefs (27 of them, in fact!). Contemporary postmodern society looks with suspicion upon any universal declarations of *what is*—and those uncomfortable with the 27 fundamental beliefs could be so because such bold assertions of truth represent an in-your-face rejection of the prevailing epistemological fuzziness of our time. Our bold proclamation of what we deem truth implicitly carries with it our bold proclamation of what we deem error, not a popular position for those those smitten by the current zeitgeist, which holds that truth is relative, contingent, and changing. (Of course, to state that truth is relative automatically rejects its counterclaim [that truth is absolute]—and thus is just as guilty of the polemics it professes to detest.)

As important as our 27 fundamental beliefs are, what's just as important is what they say about our 27 fundamental disbeliefs. Thus to be an Adventist is to express not only what we believe, but also what we don't.

—◦—

The Problem of Knowledge

"In order to assert something and mean it without qualification, I of course have to believe that it is true, but I don't have to believe that I could demonstrate its truth to all rational persons. The claim that something is universal and the acknowledgment that I couldn't necessarily prove it are logically independent of each other. The second does not undermine the first" (Stanley Fish, Harper's Magazine, July 2002, p. 34).

As an Adventist who believes that our message is true and universal (see Rev. 14:6,7) and yet can't necessarily "demonstrate its truth to all rational persons," I love Fish's quote because it affirms a thought that's been flagellating my frontal lobe for decades: *I can believe what I can't always prove,* a helpful concept for someone whose worldview is founded, at the bottom, not upon equations, formulas, axioms, and laws, but upon that most wistful (yet powerful) force among fallen creatures, and that's faith.

The Mules That Angels Ride

How does one "prove" faith? One doesn't, because if "proved," it's no longer faith.

Fish's quote knits different threads into a single issue: What does it mean to "know," as compared with "believe," something? Can fallen, subjective beings, such as ourselves ever "know" anything, or are our indubitable certainties just extreme belief, intellectual fanaticism, nothing more? Do I "know" that Jesus died for my sins any more than a suicide bomber "knows" that he's going to heaven after the explosion, or do we both just "believe" these things?

I'm dawdling here, I admit, amid the muck of Western philosophical thought regarding the question of all questions: What is knowledge? After all, how can we know something if we aren't even sure what it means to "know" anything? In fact, in studying the act of knowledge itself, we run into the problem I bumbled through in last month's column about Kurt Gödel's Incompleteness Theorem. How do I know that what I know about knowledge is right, when my very criteria for knowing anything are what are being questioned to begin with? As the apostle Paul observed: "If any man think that he knoweth any thing, he knoweth nothing yet as he ought to know" (1 Cor. 8:2).

I believe (for instance) that the sun will rise tomorrow. But what "proof" can I present? All I have, really, are past experiences of its are rising each morning and some knowledge of the laws of astronomy. But just because something happened with unceasing regularity in the past doesn't automatically mean it will happened in the future. Couldn't some unknown factor within the laws of astronomy cause the sun not to rise tomorrow? Of course, the God who created all nature could stop it from rising, couldn't He? Meanwhile, I'm aware of no logical or inherent contradiction in asserting that the sun won't rise. Thus, do I *know* the sun will rise, or do I just believe it?

In the same way, do I know that God has raised up the Seventh-day Adventist Church with a present truth message for the world, or do I just believe it? I might have many valid reasons for my position—everything from my own personal experience with the Lord (who brought me to Adventism) to the powerful testimony of the Bible (which affirms me in my Adventist belief). But having valid justification to believe something doesn't necessarily make that belief true; a person living 500 years ago at the bottom of an equatorial rain forest would have valid justification for believing that water could never be made so hard that one could walk across it, would he not?

150

The cross, Sabbath, the state of the dead, 1844, the sanctuary, all the truths in Jesus that make me an Adventist—though I can't say that I *know* them to be true (any more than I *know* the sun will rise tomorrow), I can say I *know* that I believe them to be true. And considering that "he who believes on the Son has everlasting life" (John 3:36, NKJV), maybe that's all I'll need to know, no matter my inability to "demonstrate its truth to all rational persons."

Text and Experience

Once, at a meeting with religious liberty leaders at the General Conference headquarters, a member of a faith that used "fishy flirting" (a euphemism for sex as an evangelistic tool) told his conversion story.

James explained that the head of the group, Moses David, had tried unsuccessfully to reach him with "the gospel." "But then," James said, "Moses David gave me his wife for the night—and that's when I learned about the love of Jesus." (When I told an American Jewish Moonie in Brazil [you meet some strange folk in religious liberty work] that Moses David gave this man his wife, the Moonie's reply was "Which one?")

After mulling over James's testimony and trying to make it fit into my own worldview, I realized—more clearly than ever—how untrustworthy experience alone can be. Though a faith whose greatest command is to "love the Lord thy God with all thine heart" (Deut. 6:5), must of necessity be experiential, that experience must be tested. After all, people who talk to the "dead," or have visions of the virgin Mary have all had experiences. The question is How do you interpret what the experience is and, more important, what does it means?

Though our common answer, that we test it through the Bible, is correct, different people have different interpretations of the Bible, often contradictory. The Lord, however, has not left us in a lurch, not here, not with something so important. In fact, He has made it abundantly easy to interpret our experiences.

For myself, who first came to Christ on experience alone, I know that my interpretation of that experience—which eventually led me to the

Seventh-day Adventist Church—was right because of one teaching in particular: the Sabbath. This truth, anchored so clearly in the Word, validated not just my experience, but my interpretation of it as well.

Think about it. Nothing we believe, as Adventists or even Christians, makes any sense apart from the fact that we have been created by God. What does Christ's death mean if our origins weren't in a loving Creator? What can salvation be in an atheistic universe? From what and for what are we saved if God didn't make us? Apart from the biblical account of origins, what is the Second Coming other than a myth akin to Orpheus's descent to the underworld? What can grace, reconciliation, and justification be if our origins are not in a God who, by virtue of His creatorship, bestows upon us grace, reconciliation, and justification? Creation literally is the foundation upon which everything we believe rests. And with that foundation gone, the structure crumbles.

That's why the first words of the Bible aren't about Christology, eschatology, or justification; they're about creation, the truth from which all these other truths spring and derive their meaning. And of the Ten Commandments, the first one even alluded to in the Creation account is the Sabbath (Gen. 2:1-3)—the only one anchored in the act of creation itself. Meanwhile, at the other end of the Bible, using language reflective of the fourth commandment, the first angel's message—with its call to "worship him that made heaven, and earth, and the sea, and the fountains of waters" (Rev. 14:7)—points to that same act of creation, showing its relevance now as well as in antiquity.

Therefore, however real their experience with Christ, Christians who reject the biblical Sabbath cut themselves off from the foundation of all their doctrine. And those Adventists who deem it intellectually sophisticated to downplay the Sabbath as a distinguishing mark have simply blinded themselves. The Sabbath isn't about a day; it's about the essence of all Christian beliefs and doctrines—the reason its usurpation by pagan Sunday is such a monumental issue.

No question, the Sabbath is of prime importance. And that's why allegiance to it proves allegiance to the God who created it, and everything else as well. Because it's so clearly depicted in Scripture, the Sabbath assures that the interpretation of the experiences that have made us Adventists is, indeed, the correct one.

It's a nice assurance to have, especially when experience may be so deceiving that even adultery can be construed as "the love of Jesus."

～

The Forms
of Truth

Four centuries before Christ, the Greek philosopher Plato expounded the doctrine of the *forms*—changeless, eternal, and nonmaterial essences or patterns that are poorly reflected by the things of this world. The circles and triangles we see, he taught, are merely copies of the perfect circle and the perfect triangle. Even the beautiful—from music to colors—are beautiful only because they share in the form of beauty.

According to Plato, we are like people who have always been chained to face a wall inside a cave; the only reality we see is shadows on the wall cast from objects outside in the sunlight. In order to see the real and perfect world, the world of the forms, we have to turn away from the wall and step into the light itself. For Plato, this could be done only through education.

Though many people (including his famous student Aristotle) have criticized Plato's metaphysics, and though Plato never quite explained where these perfect forms existed (the "mind of God," perhaps?), the theory of forms presents a powerful analogy regarding Christ and His church. The absolute perfection that supposedly existed in the forms exists, instead, in Jesus, the literal embodiment of perfection. And, as a church, we are to reflect that perfection. That we don't, of course, is understood; that our failure does not take away from Christ's perfection and the perfect truth that comes from Him should, indeed, be even more understood.

No matter how many blunders we as a church commit, no matter how many errors the local conference or even the General Conference itself makes, the truth in Christ remains unaltered. In the same sense that Plato's world of the forms stayed unaffected by the world's faulty reflections of it, the truth that Christ has given this church remains unaffected by the faulty manner in which the church attempts to live and teach that truth.

American poet Walt Whitman once wrote, "Only what proves itself to every man and woman is so, /Only what nobody denies is so." More erroneous words could have never been penned. What is so is so—regardless of what any man or woman believes or denies.

What do I mean? If, for example, every seventh-day Sabbathkeeper in the world started keeping Sunday, would that nullify the seventh-day

Sabbath? Does the validity of that truth depend, in any way, on how many people keep it or the quality of their obedience? Even more important, is that truth in any way implicated by the moral character of those who keep it? If Hitler had been a Sabbathkeeper, would that invalidate the Sabbath truth? Of course not.

If Christ entered the Second Apartment of the heavenly sanctuary in 1844 to begin the pre-Advent judgment, then all the books, tapes, articles, and sermons written or preached against it don't change that reality. Even if the Seventh-day Adventist Church were (as some within our ranks wish) to utterly disassociate itself from that belief, it would make no difference, at least to the truth itself. That truth, or any other truth in Christ, can no more be changed, weakened, or nullified by human actions than can a unanimous vote by a General Conference session that the sun not rise keep the sun from rising.

We must distinguish the message from the messengers. The truths we believe are perfect truths, even if we understand and proclaim them imperfectly. Even more important, the truths we have as Seventh-day Adventists remain that way, whatever we as individual Seventh-day Adventists do or even what the church as a whole does.

All who are members of this church at some point have to ask themselves a crucial question: Why am I a Seventh-day Adventist? Answers such as Because the people are loving or Because I was raised that way or Because I like the food aren't good enough. What first drew you here doesn't matter (maybe it was the food); what matters is why you remain. Anything short of a Holy Spirit-inspired conviction—born out of prayer, obedience, and study of the Word—that we have been given sacred eternal truths that no one else is preaching will leave you staring only at the cave wall, while the light of truth shines brightly outside your view.

—∞—

The Pythagoras Factor

About five centuries before Christ a Greek mystic and mathematician named Pythagoras started his own denomination. Pythagoras believed in, among other things, the transmigration of souls after death. They were strict vegetarians who refused to eat beans, who believed that couples should make love only in winter, that disciples should always put their right sandal on before the left, and that one should never eat food that drops from the table.

The core of their faith, however, could be found in the phrase "All is number." For Pythagoreans, reality—from musical tones to the motion of stars—could be reduced to simple ratios expressed in the basic formula of a/b (a and b being nice, neat whole integers, such as 1, 2, 4, 50, and so forth).

However, the theological foundation of Pythagoreanism was shattered by the discovery of irrationals, numbers that cannot be expressed as ratios involving only integers. One example is the square root of two, which comes out to 1.41421356237309504880168872420969807856967187537 6948073176 . . . and so on, without ever repeating itself. To make matters worse, far from being some abstract mathematical concepts without existence, irrationals were found in the most basic structures of nature, including squares and circles.

With their theological universe shattered, Pythagoreans were sworn to secrecy regarding irrationals; those who violated that oath were disfellow-shipped or (according to legend) suffered even worse fates.

I use the Pythagoreans (however wacky an example) to make a point about the right of religion to identify the parameters of its faith, whatever those parameters are and whatever the rationale—"good" or (as with the Pythagoreans) "bad"—behind them.

A church, any church, must define itself, must identify what it is, what it believes in, what it stands for. By so doing, it by default identifies what it *isn't,* what it *doesn't* believe in, and what it *doesn't* stand for. The tough question is How much deviation from these definitions can a church allow before losing its identity?

Should, for instance, a person be allowed in the Seventh-day Adventist ministry, or on an Adventist theology faculty, who doesn't believe in God? Or who rejects the Messiahship of Jesus? Or who believes that Jesus never rose from the dead? Or who is an avowed satanist? Even the most "tolerant" of us would not want someone with any of these views in our pulpits or before our classrooms.

Of course, once they agree that an atheist or a satanist shouldn't be an Adventist theology teacher or pastor, they agree that the church does have the right to close its pulpits and classrooms to those it deems outside certain theological parameters.

Though satanists and atheists are easy ones, what about someone who doesn't accept a literal six-day Creation? Or who teaches that Daniel was written in the second century B.C. as opposed to the sixth? Should we have to allow someone on a theology faculty who accepts only 24 of the 27 fundamentals? Or maybe only 16 or 12 or 3? Where's the cutoff point, because clearly there must be one somewhere (after all, one of the fundamentals deals with belief in God Himself)?

By defining the parameters of its faith, the church automatically excludes what doesn't fit within them. To proclaim Jesus as Messiah is, by default, to place outside our parameters all stances that reject Jesus as the Messiah. To believe that God created the world in six literal 24-hour days means to reject all contradictory views (such as theistic evolution and so forth).

Again, what Adventist will tolerate an avowed satanist in one of our pulpits preaching nude moonlight dance rituals or the use of black magic? But what about someone who rejects the sixth-century date of Daniel, or a worldwide flood, or the pre-Advent judgment beginning in 1844? For me it's hard to understand why one who rejects those teachings would even *want* to be an Adventist, much less teach or preach among us. But the issue isn't if they want to; the issue is Should they even be allowed to (that is, teach or preach among us)?

Our leaders and administrators not only must define the parameters of our faith; they have the right—even the obligation—to enforce them.

To do anything else would be, well, irrational.

‑‑‑

The Pythagoras Factor—Again

Most columnists (I imagine) have faced this paradox: you pen (what you deem) a provocative, in-your-face piece that ultimately elicits only long dry yawns. In contrast, during an intellectual and creative torpor, you hack out what feels obvious, even bland, and you incite outrage. The latter depicts what happened with "The Pythagoras Factor" (July 26, 2001), in which I expressed a position whose apparentness was (I thought) axiomatic to the point of boorishness: that a volunteer organization, such as our church, had the right, even the duty, to be sure that its teachers and preachers believed what we as a church claim to believe.

Hardly an epochal or pioneering notion, to be sure. However—judging by the cascade of angry letters, by the fulminations and diatribes against me on the Internet, by an article in an independent journal lambasting my position, and by a rancorous tongue-lashing in the hallowed halls of the General Conference—it's obvious that some not only rejected my position (that our preachers and teachers should believe what we as a church believe), but thought it outrageous.

Perhaps, though, the problem wasn't the point, but the weaknesses with which I expressed it. Thus I'll try again, but from another angle.

Let's begin with an Adventist dad. We'll call him George. Now George is, as most Adventists are, fairly conservative, and he sends junior off to an Adventist college under the assumption that junior will be taught Adventist beliefs, such as those found in our 27 fundamental doctrines. Among them, George would expect that the teachers would believe in the Bible as "the infallible revelation of His [God's] will" (no. 1), that "in six days the Lord made 'the heaven and the earth'" (no. 6), and that the gift of prophecy "was manifested in the ministry of Ellen G. White" (no. 17).

Though George realizes that a certain amount of disagreement is not only inevitable but good, especially in an academic environment, is it asking too much for George to expect that the teachers—with whom he's trusting his child—would themselves be committed to these and other Adventist beliefs? Does not basic honesty (much less decency) demand that teachers who didn't believe this way should at least let George know beforehand, so that he could make a well-informed decision about his child's education? If comfortable sending junior into an environment where, for instance, the teachers worked from the premises of higher criticism, or they believed in theistic evolution, or they rejected the prophetic gift of Ellen White—then George could do just that. But to send his child to a college assuming (or even being led to believe) that this child is being taught one thing while, overtly or subtly, he's being taught another is the height of intellectual dishonesty.

Whatever our cognoscenti mean by "academic freedom," they surely don't think it means the right to deceive poor George, do they?

George knows there are unsolved questions about his Adventist faith (if there weren't, why would we call it "faith"?); and George knows that at the college level students need to be exposed to these questions in a candid and honest manner. But shouldn't George expect these questions to be presented by teachers who have not only worked them through in their own minds and experiences, but who can then convey their faith, and their best answers, to his son in a way that affirms junior's Adventism rather than weakens it? Should George expect anything less?

Also, wouldn't George's son be better off in a classroom with a teacher who openly expressed disbelief in our teaching rather than with one teaching what he or she didn't really believe? Students aren't stupid: no matter what's said in the classroom, it doesn't take long for them to know where the teacher really stands on these issues. Shouldn't George, who's paying big bucks for his son's education, have the assurance that those who teach his child Adventist beliefs actually believe them themselves, rather than just spouting the party line in order to keep their jobs?

My point in "The Pythagoras Factor" is simply this: Our colleges need to be honest with the parents who entrust them with their offspring.

Hardly a radical notion, is it?

One wouldn't think so.

─◈─

Seventh-day Darwinians

R arely has there been a belief so ridiculous or contrary to the Scriptures that, once it becomes popular, some Christians haven't attempted to incorporate it into the faith. In its long and often crude lust for cultural and intellectual correctness, the church has become what Jacques Ellul called "an empty bottle that the successive cultures fill with all kinds of things." Roman paganism, Platonism, Marxism, even Nazism have all had baptized aficionados struggling to cram these "things" into the bottle, now so warped and piecemeal it resembles a kaleidoscope image inspired by someone needing Prozac.

Of all the bizarre mismatches, though, none's worse than the attempt to harmonize evolution with Christianity. Evolution? Please! Nazism's a snugger fit.

Though raised on evolution, I one day found myself a born-again Christian who saw, immediately, an impossible conundrum between what I was taught my whole life and my new worldview. Within the first few days someone gave me the book *The Genesis Flood,* by Henry Morris, and for the first time I realized that the "proof" I was dogmatically given for evolution wasn't as solid as I had been led to believe from grade school through college. Over time, and after more reading, I was soon purged of all macroevolutionary presuppositions. In fact, if (heaven forbid) I ever lost my faith, I could never go back to evolution. Alien seeding or the Babylonian creation story seems more plausible than the standard scientific paradigm of origins.

"But," someone would say, "it's science." Exactly. And science is still only a human endeavor, and as such it comes burdened with all the prejudices, foibles, fears, and presuppositions of anything human. However much I respect science and stand in awe of its achievements, scientists can be as bigoted and dogmatic as historical critics (well, almost).

Now, it used to be that, for Adventists, evolutionary theory was a threat from without; as unbelievable as it seems, some among us have now accepted theistic evolution—the idea that God used the process of evolution, over millions of years, to create humanity.

These folks, though, don't worship the God of the Bible, for that God didn't use a long, protracted, and vicious dog-eat-dog, survival-of-the-fittest paradigm—one that goes against everything He has taught us about love and self-sacrifice—and then lie to us about it by claiming He created life here in six days when He didn't. Plus, that God didn't ask us to keep the seventh day as a memorial, not to the six days of Creation as He explicitly told us in His Word, but to a brutal, hateful, merciless process that took millions of years.

What amazes me isn't so much that people can believe in evolution (after all, I used to), but that those who do still want to be Seventh-day Adventists. I can respect someone who, believing in evolutionary theory, rejects the Adventist Church entirely. I have no respect for those who think they can meld the two.

For anyone, especially our young people, struggling with these issues, I say: Keep seeking with a fervent and honest heart. As long as you stick to the Bible (and Ellen White's books and articles) you will not go wrong. For those among us who have already decided—despite the Bible and Ellen White—on evolution, there are plenty of other churches for you. Ours isn't one. And to those teaching in our schools who believe in evolution and yet take a paycheck from the Seventh-day Adventist Church, I say: If you honestly reject a literal six-day creation in favor of theistic macroevolution, fine; now turn that honesty into integrity and go somewhere where you won't have to cloak your views under the anfractuosities of language.

I speak, I believe, for millions of Seventh-day Adventists when I declare that whatever the age of the earth itself, we will *never* make room for anything other than a literal six-day creation for life here—never. And for those who want more, you'll have to fight us for every extra minute—much less your millions of mythological years beyond—of which the Word of God knows nothing and with its first verses utterly denies.

-~-

Defining
Down Deviancy

I once sat on a committee in which a member, an ordained Seventh-day Adventist minister, argued that "as a denomination we should accept monogamous, practicing homosexuals as full church members."

Though after an embarrassed silence the committee ignored the statement and continued its work, those words represent what has been termed "defining down deviancy"—meaning simply that our nation's moral fiber has declined so greatly that the once unacceptable is now, if not right, at least not considered worthy of rebuke, shame, or reproach. In other words, the culture is so steeped in sin that it no longer seems sinful, and those who label it as such are "Victorian bigots."

Just how far have we defined down deviancy?

Last year a Hawaiian court ruled in favor of gay marriages. No wonder. With homosexual practice now merely an "alternative lifestyle," with elementary school textbooks titled *Heather Has Two Mommies,* and with homosexual characters portrayed on TV, who should be surprised that gay marriages could soon be legally sanctioned?

Had Bill Clinton been running for office in the era of John F. Kennedy, he might never have politically survived the moral scandals that many Americans (including me) today are apparently willing to shrug off.

During the past presidential campaign Bob Dole cited *True Lies,* with Arnold Schwarzenegger (a movie containing nearly 100 killings!) as one film "most friendly to the family."

Milos Forman's *The People vs. Larry Flynt* turned the five-times married, drug-addicted publisher of the vile, racist, scatological porn magazine *Hustler* into an American hero and defender of free speech and human rights.

Churchy Things

How can all this happen? The answer is easy. We have defined down deviancy.

Why? Though many factors are involved, the problem stems partly from the pervasiveness of postmodernism, which teaches that concepts as truth and morality, right and wrong—even up and down—don't exist in any objective, absolute sense; but only as relative, indeterminate, fluctuating notions that each individual and community must define for themselves. Unlike the modern world's belief in an objective reality that could be understood by human reason, postmodernism rejects the very notion of objectivity itself, a position that inevitably leads to moral chaos.

After all, if objective truth doesn't exist, then objective morality doesn't either. Standards of right and wrong, good and evil, truth and error, aren't rooted in any absolute—whether God, natural law, divine law, or even tradition—but are only what either individuals or the community decides, and if the community doesn't see premarital sex or homosexuality or pornography as wrong, then they aren't wrong, because there's no absolute to say they are.

Yet the postmodern premise is inherently self-contradictory, because to state that no objective truth exists is in and of itself an attempt to state objective truth.

The fact, of course, is that objective truth does exist, and it's rooted in Jesus Christ, the one in whom "we live, and move, and have our being" (Acts 17:28). No matter how much our culture denies or ignores them, absolute standards of right and wrong are real, and society can no more by majority rule eradicate them than it can by majority rule vote God out of existence.

And for this reason our nation groans from substance abuse, sexually transmitted diseases, corruption, mental illness, broken homes, teen pregnancy, crime—everything. The society is being destroyed by the very sin that it denies even exists. You don't have to believe in God's law to suffer the inevitable consequences of violating it, any more than denying the existence of gravity will stop you from falling when you leap off a bridge.

Ideas, it has been said, have consequences. Postmodernism is an idea, defining down deviancy a consequence. On American primetime TV, for example, only 6 percent of the sexual acts are between married partners. And our nation bemoans teen pregnancy?

Defining down deviancy hasn't pervaded just our society, as the committee member's words indicate—it's not only reached the church door; it's in the pew and pulpit as well.

Illegal Lefts
and Liberty

MY ONE PAGE a month began with the *Review* in 1996, when I was still editor of *Liberty*. I was to write a column about religious liberty and last-day events, which I did for a number of years, until—after deciding that I didn't want to spend the rest of my life bashing Jerry Falwell—I quit *Liberty* and moved on. Fortunately, the *Review* let me keep my column; even better, I wasn't limited to the previous themes. I could go in just about any direction. By the time of the transition, however, I had already done a few years' worth of columns on religious liberty and last-day events. This final section is composed of those columns (plus a few later ones on the same topics). In them I deal with everything from the time I almost got in a fight with Nazis in front of the White House to more elevated issues such as Michael Foucalt's criticism of all power structures as "regimes of truth." Plus, I looked at the question of religious freedom and last-day events in post 9/11 America. As expected, many of these pages were controversial (talking about politics *and* religion together, come on!). And though limited by the topics themselves, I again always strove with these pages, to the degree they allowed, to affirm us in Truth, at least the best that I understood it at the time.

We do grow, after all, don't we?

The Risks of Love

For years physicists have been seeking a "theory of everything" (TOE), a complete description of the world defined by a neat mathematical formula. They have so far failed because, though a TOE exists, it's not written in numbers; it's written blood, the blood of Christ—and its message is simply *"God is love"* (1 John 4:8).

Because God is love, He created us with the capacity to love as well. Yet love, by its very definition, can't be coerced; love—to be love—must allow the option *not* to love. Inherent in love, therefore, is freedom, and freedom involves risks. For God, love was worth that risk, even at the cost of a crown of thorns on the head of His crucified Son.

At the heart of the gospel, then, is love, and at the heart of love, liberty. The cross proves just how sacred that liberty is: had God not granted it to us, we would not have sinned, would not have broken His law, and Jesus Christ wouldn't have had nails in His hands and feet, and the sins of the world on His back.

The principle of religious freedom isn't limited only to the earth. In *Early Writings* Ellen White wrote of a vision she had of life on another planet: "Then I saw two trees. . . . The fruit of both looked beautiful, but of one they [the inhabitants] could not eat. They had power to eat of both, but were forbidden to eat of one. Then my attending angel said to me, 'None in this place have tasted of the forbidden tree; but if they should eat, they would fall'" (p. 40). Here, as in Eden, the power, the option, to disobey must exist; otherwise, love couldn't either.

During His earthly ministry Jesus exemplified the freedom inherent in love. Just as the Father never forced love or obedience in heaven (otherwise, how could Lucifer and the angels have rebelled?), Jesus never forced

163

it on earth. When Jesus told the rich young ruler what he needed to do to be saved, the ruler walked away. Though Jesus knew the consequences of that decision, and though He loved the man—indeed, because He loved the man—He didn't force the issue. Jesus wept for souls, pleaded for their salvation, admonished them to have eternal life through Him, but He never, either in heaven or earth, trampled upon the sacred right of religious freedom. To do so would violate a law of His own creating.

America's Founders understood this principle. Thomas Jefferson wrote that God, "being Lord both of body and mind," chose "not to propagate it [religion] by coercions on either, as was in His Almighty power to do." In other words, though God has the power to force us to obey, He doesn't.

The genius of the American experiment was to establish a government based on freedom of choice regarding religion (reflective somewhat of the freedom God granted in His government). According to prophecy, however, the experiment fails. The United States, repudiating the principles of freedom, will actually coerce religious worship: "And [it] causeth the earth and them which dwell therein to worship the first beast, whose deadly wound was healed" (Rev. 13:12).

Though the real issue in the great controversy between Christ and Satan deals with God's character and the justness of His government, the battle climaxes around the more mundane question of religious liberty and freedom to worship.

Thus, because religious liberty is so fundamental, not only to the gospel itself but to last-day events, the *Review* has asked me to write about religious liberty issues in the context of the three angels' messages. What is religious liberty? How is it being threatened? How do we interpret the news in the light of Bible prophecy? How could the United States ever fulfill its prophetic role? These are just a few of the many questions we will explore.

But I need your help: send me clips on religious liberty topics, particularly any that you think could be of relevance to our understanding of last-day events.

We should all be interested in religious liberty, not just because of the scenario that precedes Christ's second coming, but because it was inherent in the principle that led Him to the cross at the first coming—and that principle, the grand TOE of the universe, is simply *God is love.*

Eternal Moral Principles

Defending against charges of human rights abuses, Chinese president Jiang Zemin said during his visit to the United States last year, "The theory of relativity worked out by Mr. Einstein, which is in the domain of natural science, I believe can also be applied to the political field. Both democracy and human rights are relative concepts and not absolute and general."

With all due respect, President Jiang ought to stick to politics, not science. Einsteinian (special) relativity is, in fact, based on the immutability and universality of the laws of physics, which remain the same in all frames of reference in uniform motion.

Nevertheless, Jiang did raise an interesting point: Is there a universal moral code applicable to all people and nations, and if so, where must it come from?

The answer, of course, depends on your view of where we come from. If, indeed, we live in a totally materialistic universe, the result of blind forces alone, then the Chinese president has a point.

After all, who decides that one culture, moral code, or form of government is better than another? Herodotus wrote about one society in which offspring were morally obligated to eat the flesh of their dead fathers. In ancient India widows often immolated themselves on the funeral pyres of their deceased husbands. Hammurabi decreed that if the daughter of a gentleman dies as a result of being struck while pregnant, then the daughter of the striker should be killed. In ancient Rome unwanted babies were left out in the elements to die.

Now, if there are no universal moral principles that exist "above," or even prior to, humankind, what gives us in the twentieth-century Western world the right to pass judgment upon these acts, no matter how repugnant they might seem? If good and bad, right and wrong, and other moral ideals are found not in God or in some eternal transcendence, but only in humanity itself—then morality is subjective, like a preference for the Spice Girls over Beethoven, or French bread over bagels. Some argue—quite logically, given their naturalistic premises—that we can't "know" right and wrong (as we "know" 2 + 2=4), because right and wrong are mere arbitrary expressions based on emotional and cultural biases.

165

On the other hand, if a moral God has established a moral universe, then concepts of absolute right and wrong, good and evil, must exist apart from humanity and its own preferences. (Though some try to base morality in natural law, just about everything has been "justified" using natural law arguments.) Far from being nothing but what J. Fishkin calls "expressions of preference . . . attitudes or feelings," moral principles—rooted in God—apply to everyone everywhere. This means that certain practices—no matter how traditional, cultural, or long-running—are right or wrong because a universal standard exists to judge them.

Of course, the belief in moral absolutes doesn't solve humanity's moral problems. For centuries people have stabbed, burned, shot, and imprisoned fellow human beings—all in the name of defending transcendent moral absolutes. Jesus Himself warned, "They shall put you out of the synagogues: yea, the time cometh, that whosoever killeth you will think that he doeth God service" (John 16:2).

The other problem, unique to the American experiment of separation of church and state, is this: If moral absolutes can exist only in the Creator, how can we incorporate these absolutes, or at least the principles reflected by them, into our society without violating separation of church and state? If moral principles emanate from God, what happens to those who don't believe in God, or whose view of His moral absolutes differs from others? Besides, what is the "mark of the beast" other than an attempt to enforce "eternal" moral principles upon those whose eternal moral principles differ from those of the majority?

President Jiang is wrong: moral absolutes do transcend cultures and nations. The challenge is determining not only what those absolutes are, but which ones should be enforced; and then finding a fair and equitable way of enforcing them on those whose moral values come from some source other than the true one.

~

Pretty Scary Folk

Those who feel called of God can sometimes be pretty scary folk. After all, when the Lord beckons, mundane things like tradition, moral norms, social stigma, friendship, loyalty and even laws are often discarded, because, answering to a higher—indeed the highest—authority, these people can let nothing interfere.

Yet even scarier than those who sense the call of God are those who sense it to effect political change. It's one thing to believe the Lord has beckoned you to feed the poor or to keep the Sabbath; it's another to hear the Lord's call to liberate the poor through armed revolution or to force others to keep a day holy.

Why? Because by their very natures, methodologies, and premises, politics and religion make a volatile and dangerous mix.

First, politics as a human institution, almost always involves compromise; in fact, it couldn't function without it. Religion, on the other hand, is based on the assumption that it comes from God, and thus it doesn't lend itself well to the give-and-take that permeates politics. To do so would mean a weakening of God-given absolutes.

Second, most reasonable politicians realize that neither they nor their leaders nor even the system they espouse are perfect, that they don't have all the answers, and that they aren't the panacea for every human ill. In contrast, religious zealots usually believe that even if they themselves don't have all the answers, the God that guides them and the religious system their God initiated does—an assumption that doesn't allow for the kind of eclecticism crucial to political discourse.

Therefore, to mix the fervor and absolutism of religion with the subjectivism and uncertainties of politics is like having a Hezballah suicide bomber as mayor.

A perfect example comes from seventeenth-century England and the reign of Lord Protector Oliver Cromwell, who led the parliamentary forces against King Charles I in the English civil war. After routing the king's forces (and signing his death warrant), Cromwell took the reins of power in 1653, and ruled until his death in 1658.

From the beginning Cromwell believed he was God's chosen instrument to save England and Protestantism, a modern-day Moses called of the Lord to bring His people to the Promised Land. Though he did allow some religious liberty, his fervent belief that God had called him to bring political and moral reform led Cromwell to rule as a dictator. He imprisoned people without trial. He taxed by decree. He would trample on the most basic rights, the whole time justified in his actions, he believed, by God's approval.

"By executing Charles, Cromwell cut himself off from justifications of political authority rooted in the past," explains *The Oxford History of*

Britain. "His self-justification lay in the future, in the belief that he was fulfilling God's will. But because he believed that he had such a task to perform, he had a fatal disregard for civil and political liberties. To achieve the future promised by God, Cromwell governed arbitrarily."

But who could blame him? As a Puritan, Cromwell was no doubt closer to the truth than either the Anglicans or the Catholics. Therefore, how could he let subjective things like civil and political liberties stand in the way of his divine mandate? The answer, of course, was that he couldn't—which is why he didn't.

Though mingled with each other of necessity, at least to a degree (after all, religious people do function in political societies), religion and politics are best kept as separate as possible. The leader, utterly sure he or she is answering the call of God, is not likely to allow the prodding of conscience or common civility to dissuade his or her actions. No wonder religious people, especially in the area of politics, have committed everything from murder, torture, rape, and brigandage to bombing clinics and shooting abortion providers—with nary a twinge of guilt. Why should anyone feel guilty about doing God's will?

Though religious fervor itself can create some pretty scary folk (David Koresh, Jim Jones, Marshall Herff Applewhite, for examples), history shows that religious zeal—when mixed with politics—has a habit of creating the scariest folk of all.

The Tyranny of the Majority

However proud Americans are of their democracy, it's a lousy way to run a country (Churchill called it the "worst form of government except all those other forms that have been tried from time to time").

First, democracy and liberty are not synonymous. Just because people live under laws they vote themselves doesn't automatically make them, or the nation they live in, free. Thomas Jefferson wrote that threats to freedom "chiefly" come, not when government acts against its constituents, but when "government is a mere instrument of the major number of the constituents."

Frenchman Alexis de Tocqueville, writing about America in the

1800s, warned that democracy, far from protecting everyone's rights, often "protects those of the majority" alone. After all, African-Americans in the South lived for years under democratic rule, and yet what they experienced could hardly be called "liberty."

Next, democratic rule assumes that the masses know what's best for their nation, which is rarely the case. Plato argued that because statecraft was so complicated, why should ordinary citizens be involved in crucial decisions about topics on which they're so often blatantly ignorant? How much, for instance, does a car mechanic in Peoria or a computer programmer in Tucson know about GATT (General Agreement on Tariffs and Trade) or Federal Reserve regulations?

Another problem with democracy is that fallen human nature being what it is, people care mostly for their own immediate interests rather than those of the nation as a whole. In *The Radicalism of the American Revolution,* Gordon S. Wood wrote that many Founders became disillusioned with American democracy precisely for this reason, and thus framed the Constitution in a way that would temper "private interests" in public government.

It didn't work. Though the Founders created a republic, in which we vote in officials who then make laws for us, as opposed to a pure democracy, in which the people make the laws themselves, these officials are still at the mercy of voters who can ignominiously dump them at the polls. (Congress is kept on an especially short leash of two-year election cycles). In other words, what makes democratic government so appealing—that is, that we plebians have a voice in it—is also what makes it so bad.

For example, Congressman A knows that Bill 55, though popular with the folks in his district, is bad for America as a whole. But because his constituents will soon be at the voting booth—and his well-funded opponent openly espouses Bill 55—Congressman A votes for the bill anyway.

"Voters routinely punish lawmakers," said Timothy Penny, a Democrat who left the House in 1994, "who try to do unpopular things, who challenge them to face unpleasant truths about the budget, crime, Social Security, or tax policy. Similarly, voters reward politicians for giving them what they want—more spending for popular programs—even if it means wounding the nation in the long run by creating more debt."

The problems with democracy become pertinent in light of last-day events. In *The Great Controversy* Ellen White wrote: "Political corruption is destroying love of justice and regard for truth; and even in free America, rulers and legislators, in order to secure public favor, will yield to *the popular demand* for a law enforcing Sunday observance. Liberty of conscience, which has cost so great a sacrifice, will no longer be respected" (p. 592; italics supplied).

A "popular demand" for a Sunday law? She's depicting not a fascist or oligarchical regime, but elected officials responding to voter demands, the essence of democratic rule. Her prediction, in fact, encompasses a major flaw of popular government: a majority—unaware of the real issues and looking out for its own interests—oppressing a minority.

Of course, the Framers instituted the federal judiciary specifically to protect against the excesses of democratic rule. But the judiciary has failed before and obviously will again.

In short, democracy—instead of protecting the church from persecution—could be the mechanism that allows it to happen. And considering democracy's flaws, it's no wonder.

Personal
Moral Matters

Last year, while boarding a flight, I saw something that brought me to tears then, and still does now. A father, heavily tattooed and exuding the rough huskiness that comes from quaffing lots of hops, was saying goodbye to his boy, about 5, with eyewear as thick as telescope lenses. The father bent over the child, who, reaching up, clasped his frail arm around the thick neck and didn't want to let go. Though the boy was more unabashed, both were crying.

Obviously, this wasn't Daddy sending junior off for a weekend with Bubba and Zeyda; instead, it was a child of divorce being painfully shuffled between parents.

That scene symbolizes one nasty and brutish fact of life: we never sin in a vacuum. Whenever we transgress—even quietly, subtly, and secretly—in one way or another, even perhaps via vehicles we ourselves can't perceive, that transgression will, to some degree, hurt others. It's a principle, a law of nature even. Sin is not a private matter; on the contrary, it's a very public thing.

Which leads to the question: If sin hurts others, how much sin should the law allow? The usual refrain, of course, is "You can't legislate morality"—absolute proof that any concept, if quoted enough, can become dogma, no matter how inane.

Of course you can legislate morality. That's all that's ever legislated. The government (through whatever its legislative process happens to be) decides that certain types of actions are "wrong" and then passes laws meant to try to keep people from performing those acts. If that's not legislated morality, what is?

Legislation can't change hearts or transform character, of course. But it's not meant to. Maybe God's law forbids you from lusting after your neighbor's wife, but Caesar's doesn't (Caesar's, though, forbids you from raping her).

The question, then, is not Can morality be legislated? but What should morality be? If you have different views of right and wrong, you're going to have different views of what should or should not be legal.

Some cases are easy. Pedophilia, for example, is outlawed in America because enough citizens think it's wrong, immoral, and hurtful to children; and so they have enacted laws against it. Hence, *moral* laws.

But what about alcohol consumption? Drinking has certainly done much more damage to society—and children—than pedophilia, yet drinking is legal and pedophilia isn't. Why? Because our society views pedophilia as more morally repugnant than drinking, and has expressed that moral preference via its legal codes.

Though most Americans agree that adultery and homosexual activity are wrong, homosexuals have faced many more legal barriers than adulterers. Yet who has done more damage to homes, to families, to children—homosexuals or adulterers? The answer is adulterers by far (because they're more prevalent), even though they have faced fewer legal restraints than homosexuals ever have. The reason? Again, it's simply because our society finds homosexuality more repugnant than adultery, a moral view reflected in its laws.

Now, back to that airport scene. Suppose divorce laws in America (reflecting our moral view of that practice) had suddenly been made more stringent. Perhaps, knowing how difficult getting a divorce now was, those parents might have tried harder to save their marriage—and who knows, they might have succeeded. Or what if the marriage had fallen apart because the father was a heavy drinker? If alcohol consumption had been outlawed, he might not have indulged as much, or perhaps not at all, and the marriage might have remained intact. Or maybe the wife had an affair that she might not have had if adultery had been subject to criminal penalties.

I'm not advocating that divorce, adultery, or alcohol be made illegal, or that people won't find ways to do what they want to despite the law. What I am suggesting, however, is that the notion that government has no business getting involved in personal moral matters is a fallacy. Government is always involved in these matters to some degree or another, if for no other reason than that—as the sobbing little boy, his pain echoing down the airport walkway, so poignantly proved—personal moral matters aren't always so "personal" after all.

-∞-

Illegal Lefts
and Liberty

The county one day placed a "no left turn" sign where I always made a left turn into the General Conference parking lot. One morning, not wanting to hassle with the extra driving caused by the new prohibition, I approached the entrance, glanced to the spot where the police usually hide (waiting to catch Adventist traffic violators) and, not seeing the cruiser, I made the illegal left.

Sure enough, the cop was hiding somewhere else, and before I got out of the car, there he was, ticket book in hand. Not only did I get a $50 fine (which was bad enough)—I had to suffer the humiliation of getting it in front of my fellow General Conference employees!

Three days later, en route to work, I was sitting in the usual traffic jam on Route 29 when I decided to bolt down the bus lane and save myself 10 minutes. Sure enough, the long arm of the law was hiding in the bushes—and voilà! I got nailed for another 50 smackers (all this during the week I was to meet with my ordination committee).

Now, no matter how backed up morning traffic is on Route 29, I no longer shoot down the bus lane (though it's tempting), nor do I make illegal lefts into the parking lot. Why? Well, for the same reason I obey a lot of the other laws: simply because the government has the power *to force* me to comply.

Indeed, the essence of all earthly government is force. Civil and criminal laws are meaningless unless backed by the power of the state to enforce them, and they enforce them through coercion. I don't pay taxes out of patriotic fervor; I pay them because the Internal Revenue Service will throw me in jail if I don't. If the government only *recommended,* as opposed to *demanded,* that we obey the law, then lots of laws (especially tax ones) would be broken.

What are the police and courts for, if not to bully citizens into obeying the law? Now, there are just and unjust laws. That's not the point. The point is that even a just law is effective only to the extent to which people obey it. In many cases people obey only because the threat of punishment compels them to (though not always—after all, I don't molest children, and it's not because I fear going to jail).

America's Founders understood this principle, which is why they sought to separate religion from secular law, the idea being that religion is worthless when coerced. Because the essence of all secular law is coercion, the safest course is to separate the two.

British philosopher John Locke, who heavily influenced Thomas Jefferson, expressed it eloquently in his *Letter Concerning Toleration:* "The care of souls," he wrote, "cannot belong to the civil magistrate, because his power consists only in outward force; but true and saving religion consists in the inward persuasion of the mind, without which nothing can be acceptable to God." Locke continued: "I may grow rich in an art that I do not take delight in; I may be cured of some diseases by remedies that I have not faith in; but I cannot be saved by a religion that I distrust or a worship that I abhor."

However grandiose this principle, the rub comes in implementing it. After all, it's not so easy to separate church and state when the church exists within the state and thus, inevitably, is subject to its laws, laws that by their essence as laws are coercive.

Should people who smoke marijuana as part of their religious belief be exempted from laws that place marijuana smokers in jail? Should Christian Scientists, who don't believe in medicine or medical treatments, be exempted from laws that demand that people give their children "proper" medical attention? Should religious people who don't want to rent to unmarried couples or practicing homosexuals be exempted from housing discrimination laws? Should Adventists and Jews be exempt from laws that, under the threat of fines, close businesses on Sundays?

These are not easy questions to answer—though you can be sure that each morning, as I drive to work, I have plenty of time to ponder them.

—∽—

Nazis in the Park

The other day a Nazi spit at me—not a square-jawed, goose-stepping Nazi in spit-shiny black boots whose iron posture revealed the discipline that allowed him to murder women and children with the cold efficiency of a machine, but an unshaven, unwashed grimy Nazi whose dirty teeth and soiled clothes revealed a lack of fortitude or discipline for anything, except (no doubt) hatred.

I met the Nazi at Lafayette Park early on a Sunday morning across the street from the White House, where my 6-year-old and I rollerblade (ever since Sixteenth and Pennsylvania was closed off for security reasons, the street in front of the White House has become the hot spot in D.C. for in-line skating). This Nazi and others had slept in the park, and that morning, when I saw their placards pasted with swastikas, and slogans about Aryan Americans uniting, I skated over to one Nazi who sat on a bench.

Though I should have witnessed to him (even if my opening line would have been "Did you know that Jesus was a Jew?"), my carnal side wanted a fight instead. If, however, I came home bloodied from duking it out with Nazis in front of the White House, my wife would no longer let me take my 6-year-old there to skate, so I simply uttered a mocking laugh, and as I started to skate away, he spit at the ground before me and said, "Excuse me." Though it wasn't easy, I kept going.

"For if you love only those who love you," Jesus said, "what credit is that to you? Even tax-collectors do that" (Matt. 5:47, Phillips). A parallel principle applies to freedom, particularly religious freedom: true liberty isn't protecting religions we like or that don't offend us. Even Nazis would do that. Instead, the real test of our commitment to freedom comes when we protect faiths that we might personally find despicable.

We're only as free, it has been said, as the most hated group among us. That's true, which is why our church, over the years, has tried to protect the free exercise of religious practices that we, as Adventists, would never practice ourselves.

For example, a few years ago we signed onto a U.S. Supreme Court brief defending the right of a Caribbean cult (Santeria) in Florida to sacrifice animals as part of its worship of the god Babalu Aye. We stressed that though we "consider these practices repugnant for moral and religious reasons," unless they are deemed detrimental to public welfare, people have a right to practice them, no matter how personally offensive to others. After all, citizens in Hialeah (which passed the ordinance banning animal sacrifices) could kill animals for sport, food, convenience, or profit; they just couldn't do it for religion. "One can get Chicken McNuggets in Hialeah," the brief said, "but one may not partake of chicken roasted at a religious service of the Santeria faith." The U.S. Supreme Court ruled 9-0 (one of the few times the High Court was unanimous in a church-state decision) that the Hialeah law banning animal sacrifices was unconstitutional.

"The freemen of America," wrote James Madison, "did not wait till usurped power had strengthened itself by exercise, and entangled the question in precedents. They saw all the consequences in the principle, and they avoided the consequences by denying the principle."

Indeed, once the principle that the government can restrict any religious practice it doesn't like is established, it's not hard to see the consequences. In this case, fortunately, the High Court avoided the consequences by denying the principle. It told the city of Hialeah that our Constitution protects even the most offensive religious practices, unless the government can show an overwhelming reason this practice must be stopped. Hialeah couldn't give an overwhelming reason, and so religious freedom prevailed—not just for a cult that kills goats and chickens as part of its worship, but for all who believe that religion is too sacred to be proscribed by the government at whim.

Freedom comes with a price, which includes the protection of views, even practices, we deem repugnant. Considering what we get in return, it's worth it—even at the cost of (among other things) headless chickens in Hialeah and heartless Nazis in Lafayette Park.

Religion by Law

At 14 I spent a summer in the Florida Keys at a scuba diving camp, where on Sunday morning everyone was required to attend worship. The complaints of Robert Gewanter and me, the only Hebrew campers, were brushed aside with the answer that the services were "nondenominational." Whatever that seven-syllable word meant (I didn't know at the time), it did little to assuage my discomfort at being forced to attend worship service on Sundays, where the name "Jesus Christ" was freely used.

However, because I was determined to spend that summer among the coral reefs of the Keys—even if it meant enduring a "nondenominational" homily every Sunday morning—I never complained to my parents, who, had they known, would have instantly returned me to the kosher cloister of Miami Beach.

Now, let's contrast summer camp to public school. Unlike the camp—which I voluntarily attended—children are forced, by the weight and power of the law, to be in public schools (at least those kids whose parents can't afford private ones). Any public school-sponsored religious activity, therefore, particularly during class hours, employs the power of the law to impose religion upon all students, even those who, for whatever reason, don't want it. That's why—in order to protect these children—the courts have placed limitations on certain religious activities in public schools.

Yet, even with these limitations, children in public schools have many constitutionally protected religious freedoms.

First, children are allowed to pray before, during, and after class. No law stops them from praying at lunch, recess, or gym class. They can pray alone, in groups, and, if they don't disturb the class, even out loud.

What has been forbidden, instead, is *school-sponsored* prayer activity, which would put coercive pressure on any child who, for whatever reason, doesn't want to partake of that religious exercise.

Second, nothing in the Constitution forbids a child from reading a Bible in public schools, nor does anything forbid public schools from teaching about religion. As the Supreme Court has ruled: "It might well be said that one's education is not complete without a study of comparative religion." What has been forbidden is *school-sponsored* religious indoctrination, which, to repeat, always comes with the power of the law behind it. What Adventist parent wouldn't object, for example, if their child were taught that Jesus changed the Sabbath to Sunday, or that the dead are in heaven and hell? To avoid these problems for children of any—or even of no—faith, the courts have wisely banned public school-sponsored religious exercises or indoctrination.

Third, in public schools children are allowed to express their religious beliefs in reports, homework, or art; at the same time they are protected from any coercion by the teacher to modify those views. Students have the right to distribute religious literature (subject to the same reasonable restrictions imposed on the distribution of all nonschool literature on school grounds). Provided it doesn't become harassment, students are even allowed to witness for their faith. Religious garb, or T-shirts carrying a religious message, are also constitutionally protected. And, thanks to recent federal legislation, if the school receives federal funds and permits any non-curricular club to meet during noninstructional time, religious clubs can use school property as well.

Of course, there is the occasional story of a child hassled for saying grace over lunch, or for silently reading a Bible in class, but these incidents no more represent true church-state separation than Nazi medical experiments represent the Hippocratic oath. Instead, they are aberrations of a policy that, while hardly flawless, does protect children who otherwise would have religion—in one degree or another—forced upon them by law.

Public school is not summer camp. Be thankful, for freedom's sake, that the courts understand the difference.

—⚮—

Fire in the Belly

Since 1983 (when I was first published in *Liberty*) I had been associated, in one way or another, with the magazine until 1999, when—after six years as editor—I quit. The reasons were many: first, I was bored; second, I had lost my fire in the belly for the topic (mostly because I had read myself out of any dogmatic positions on religious liberty); and finally, I didn't want to spend the rest of my days bashing Jerry Falwell, Pat Robertson, and other ersatz ayatollahs of the Christian Right.

Last December, however, after reading an advertisement in *Christianity Today* (Dec. 4, 2000) by The American Center for Law and Justice (Pat Robertson's answer to the American Civil Liberties Union), I felt that fire rekindle, even rage.

The ad had a picture of the Declaration of Independence in which its references to "Nature's God" and to "the Creator" were crossed out, followed in huge red type by the word "Censored?" The ad warned that unless Christians fought those who want to "take God out of public life," then soon "you will not be free to pray, read your Bible, hold a Bible study in your home, display a cross, share your faith . . . or worse."

Excuse me while I vent.

First, notice that the Declaration of Independence, not the United States Constitution, was used in the ad. Why? Because if they had used the Constitution, there would have been no references to God to cross out. How embarrassing (not to mention politically inconvenient) for the Christian Right that America's founding charter not only never refers to God, but barely mentions religion; and when it does, it distinctly puts restrictions on what government can do with it. That's why the ACLJ had to substitute the Constitution with a document that has no legal authority whatsoever.

The Declaration of Independence (written by Thomas Jefferson) was simply a public statement—penned even before the United States was established—that has no more jurisdiction over our laws or government than does Mary Shelley's *Frankenstein*. (In the recent brouhaha over the 2000 presidential election, no one talked about what the Declaration of Independence said but only about what the Constitution says, because it, not the Declaration, is the law of the land.)

Second, the ad also reads: "Let us show you what Thomas Jefferson *really* had to say about God's involvement with our nation"; it then offers to send them a free copy of the Declaration of Independence (not the U.S. Constitution).

Forget, for now, what Jefferson had to say about God in public life; let's look instead at Jefferson's God. Jefferson rejected the idea that Christ died for our sins; he rejected all miracles in the Gospels; he called Christ's apostles and disciples "dupes and imposters"; he derided Paul as "the first corrupter of Jesus"; and he wrote that the virgin birth of Christ will one day "be classed with the fable of Minerva in the brain of Jupiter." If this were the God that people wanted to acknowledge publicly at high school football games or at graduation ceremonies or over school intercoms during class time, you could be sure that Robertson's ACLJ bullies would not be producing Goebbels-like ads about the Lord being censored from public life.

Which comes to the third and most important point: despite ACLJ propaganda, there is no systematic attempt by anyone credible to stop people from praying, holding Bible studies, sharing their faith, or displaying a cross—*provided that those who do these things don't use, overtly or subtly, the coercive power of the state (be it in public schools, in courtrooms, wherever) to do them.* That's the caveat that the writers of the ad conveniently ignored. The claim that attempts to stop legislated prayer in public school (where kids must be by law) will lead to a time when "you will not be free to pray" at all is like saying that laws against sex with minors will lead to a ban on the marriage bed. The first argument is as ludicrous as the second; yet the first is being promoted by Pat Robertson's minions, and millions of Christians believe it.

Distorting truth beyond belief, the ad bordered on satire. Only it wasn't funny. In fact, it was enough to almost make me wish I were back at *Liberty*.

Almost.

⁓

The Amendment Means

From the moment it flowed from the quill of Gouverneur Morris, the U.S. Constitution was severely, almost fatally, flawed—as anything conceived in such radical compromise would be. (After all, the document not only sanctioned slavery, but allowed for "the migration or importation of such persons" for almost another 20 years!)

Fortunately, the framers knew its faults (none of them were, in fact, particularly enamored with their product) and thus built within the document a means for amending it, other than armed revolt (the usual agent of radical political change). They also made the amendment process difficult. Of the 10,000-plus amendments proposed over more than 200 years, only 27 have ever made it in (and the first 10, the Bill of Rights, were done almost at once, within about two years of ratification). The difficulty was purposeful: the framers didn't want frivolous changes.

Also, the framers didn't want to leave something as crucial as constitutional amendments in the hands of the legislature alone. What could stop the House and the Senate, for example, from amending the Constitution to enable them to serve life terms? Though the Constitution itself, in its preamendment form, was antimajoritarian in that it tried to keep power away from the masses as much as possible, the amending process was one in which the masses, through their state governments, played a crucial role.

In order to make it into the Constitution, an amendment needs to be passed, not by simple majority in the House and the Senate, but a *two-thirds majority* in both. Then, however, the proposed amendment needs a *three-fourths* majority of state legislatures or conventions. Congress and the Senate could pass all the amendments they want; ultimately the people, through their states, had to approve. In other words, the basic charter of government could not be changed without the approval of the governed themselves. The framers, whatever their faults, weren't stupid.

And if Americans ever needed a reason to be glad the framers weren't, the now-defunct Religious Equality Amendment, which never got past the House, gave it to them.

Despite the name, this amendment would have radically altered and undermined all the establishment clause protections that we have enjoyed for decades.

First, the proposed amendment stated that its purpose was "to secure the people's rights to acknowledge God according to the dictates of conscience." Now, maybe I'm missing something here, but haven't Americans been acknowledging God according to the dictates of their conscience for more than 200 years now?

Second, the bill said that the right to pray in public schools "shall not be infringed." This language implies that children don't have that right, which is false. They do. What they don't have is the right to pray in school in ways that infringe upon the freedom of others, a prohibition that has been a pillar of establishment clause jurisprudence for decades, and rightly so. If passed, this amendment would have allowed majority religions impose forms of worship, prayer, and doctrine upon others in public schools.

The bill's guarantee that no person shall be required to "join in school prayer or other religious activity" was no protection, either. In numerous rulings the Supreme Court has said that merely pressuring a person, especially a child, to partake of or even be exposed to forms of worship that offend them is an establishment of religion. That a Muslim child isn't forced to pray to Jesus or to sing hymns honoring the Trinity, but is merely required—by law—to listen while the rest of the class does isn't religious freedom.

Nor is excusing the kids from the exercises an answer. As a New York *Times* editorial in 1962 said regarding *Engel v. Vitale* (the archetypical school prayer case): "The establishment clause is a keystone of American liberty: and if there is one thing that the establishment clause must mean, it is that government may not set up a religious norm from which one has to be excused—as was the case with the children in the New York school who did not wish to recite the prayer," and which also would be the case if the Religious Equality Amendment had been passed.

Fortunately, it didn't. And for that, we should thank God—and then the framers.

Common Laws
and Orders

More than three centuries ago religious liberty pioneer Roger Williams likened the ideal society to a ship filled with passengers of many faiths who were never "forced to come to the ship's prayers or worship; nor, secondly, compelled from their own particular prayers or worship, if they practice any." Fair enough, and almost everyone in America would agree.

Williams also wrote that the vessel's "Commander" had the right to force obedience to the "common laws and orders of the ship." Another reasonable assertion, except for one problem: who determines what those "common laws and orders" are? What if they clash with some passengers' religious convictions? What if some find those laws and orders morally offensive?

The problem is that in every society (Williams's ship included), law must reflect some type of moral code. Law, after all, either prohibits or promotes certain behavior, depending, of course, upon what that society deems right or wrong. In other words, morality determines law. Laws in Nazi Germany, for example, mirrored one morality, laws in apartheid South Africa another, laws in the Civil War's Confederacy another.

Thus, saying that morality shouldn't be legislated is like saying that water shouldn't be wet. Morality is always legislated. The question is Whose morality?

Until 30 or 40 years ago that was a relatively easy question to answer in America, where for much of the nation's history there existed a basic consensus regarding family, marriage, gender, sexuality—a consensus that has broken down in recent decades, as many longtime moral axioms are being questioned or even discarded.

This change can be good or bad, depending upon what has been replaced and with what. After all, in the same parts of America where pornography was forbidden, so were integrated schools. Kids today might be having sex too young, but at least they're not forced to work torturous 16-hour days in sweatshops.

Yet for the most part, the change has been bad, and many people recognize it. Said *Newsweek,* "The fraying of America's social fabric—once considered the crotchety preoccupation of the cultural right—has become a national (even liberal) obsession."

Though everyone—from Hillary Clinton to Pat Robertson—might agree that we're turning into a society of moral degenerates, Hillary and Pat don't always agree on just what is "moral" or "degenerate" (for example, Hillary's "right to choose" is Pat's "infanticide"). And that makes finding a solution to this moral crisis difficult.

The much-touted "culture war" arises, not because most passengers on the ship are trying to coerce worship or prayers (except for those who want to legislate it in public schools); instead, the battle comes because the passengers radically disagree over what kind of "common laws and orders" the "Commander" should enforce.

If the ship were a totalitarian regime, the laws would come from the top down, and either you obeyed or were deep-sixed. In the American republic, however, power comes from below, from the passengers themselves, who are so diverse in their moral and religious views that they can't agree on what those "common laws and orders" should be.

Inevitably some sort of moral/legal parameters must be drawn for a society to survive. Who draws them, and where? That's the big struggle, especially now. Because in America people disagree not only over moral assumptions, but even over the very methods and principles used to derive those assumptions.

As Adventists, we know where it will all end. Chuck Colson—a force behind the uniting of Protestants and Catholics into a political bloc—once wrote about those like himself who were "committed to the moral order of the universe as God has established it."

Fine, except for one slight technicality: they don't understand what that moral order is. After all, if they can't even get the Ten Commandments right, who's going to trust them with something as metaphysical as "the moral order of the universe"?

Thus it won't be fun to be on board when they write their mistaken views into the "common laws and orders." In fact, they'll sink the ship entirely.

Off Their Pedestal

A round the corner from my office, on a single pedestal, sit the busts of James Madison and Thomas Jefferson, the two architects of possibly America's greatest philosophical contribution to humanity: the principle of religious freedom.

Yet the two icons don't always engender respect: depending on the occasion, someone places party hats (birthdays), rabbit ears (Easter), or Santa caps (Christmas) on them. Other times the two Founders have been adorned with clerical collars and even Groucho Marx noses and glasses. (What those touring the General Conference complex think is anyone's guess).

It's all, of course, done in good fun, and not meant to depreciate Madison's or Jefferson's enduring contribution to religious liberty. At the same time, however, the jesting can be a reminder that these men weren't perfect, even in their views of religious liberty. In fact, Thomas Jefferson once wrote a Sunday law bill that James Madison pushed through the Virginia legislature! That's right! The same men who established the principles so crucial to freedom also egregiously violated those principles by promoting a law to punish "Sabbath breakers."

What happened is this: After the Colonies declared independence from England in 1776, legislators in Virginia wanted to rewrite state laws, harmonizing them with republican principles and stripping away, as much as they deemed appropriate, vestiges of the British monarchy. The result was the revision of 126 state laws, of which Jefferson revised 46, including three of the five laws that dealt with religion.

Nothing happened to the revisions until the mid-1780s, a few years after the Revolutionary War ended. At that time Jefferson was the American minister in France, so James Madison—by then a powerful and respected Virginia politician—pushed most of the bills through the Virginia legislature, including Jefferson's Bill 84, A Bill For Punishing Disturbers of Religious Worship and Sabbath Breakers (notice the religious language of the bill: it wanted to punish *"Sabbath* Breakers").

How could Thomas Jefferson, who helped establish the eternal principles of religious liberty, advocate the punishment of Sabbath breakers? How could James Madison, such a staunch separationist—even opposing chaplains for the military and tax breaks for churches—push the bill through the legislature?

We don't know. Neither man left to posterity their motives for the Sunday law. The best we can do is offer a few possible explanations.

First, however egregious the bill, it was a revision of an earlier, much stricter Sunday law that actually prohibited travel on Sunday (except to and from church)—a provision missing from Jefferson's more liberal version.

Second, people just didn't understand the principles of religious liberty back then. (For example, it took Jefferson almost a decade to get his famous Bill for Establishing Religious Freedom through the Virginia legislature). Though Jefferson and Madison might have seen the inconsistency of Sunday legislation with religious liberty protections, they might have known that Virginians—who carried these laws over from England (Virginia was a heavily Anglican colony)—weren't ready for anything as radical as abolishing them.

Third, perhaps the most important factor was that because the colony was inhabited mostly by Protestants and Catholics (there were a few Jews, but they didn't have any rights to speak of) the issue aroused no controversy. Everyone, to some degree, already kept Sunday.

Of course, we can speculate about Jefferson's Sunday law until the cows come home, but the unfortunate historical fact remains: the two founders of religious freedom in America worked to establish the one thing Adventists fear the most. And if that weren't bad enough, the U.S. Supreme Court in the 1960s used Madison's support for the bill to help justify the Court's decision to uphold the constitutionality of Sunday laws.

The lesson from this is simple: history the Founders (even pillars like Madison and Jefferson) aren't necessarily kind to our positions. Fortunately, they don't need to be, because our positions are based on the Word of God and the life and teaching of Jesus, not on American history or even the life and teaching of Madison and Jefferson—a fact that the occasional party hat or even Groucho Marx glasses can help remind us of.

The Myth of Separation?

Denying that anyone can objectively view history, French philosopher Michael Foucalt argued that all unifying historical theories were nothing but "regimes of truth" that seek to legitimize political power. For Foucalt, history had no meaning, and those who gave it meaning did so only to validate present structures. In other words, those who control our understanding of our past, he warned, would control our future as well.

Though Foucalt (who died in 1984) was too extreme, he had a point—and it can best be seen in the current battle over the "Christian" origins of America. In its quest for political power, the Christian Right is rewriting America's past—and the most egregious offender is David Barton, whose revisionism does to American history what the Holocaust deniers do to Jewish history.

Barton's premise is simple: separation of church and state was never what America's founders intended. He even wrote a book, called *The Myth of Separation,* that says: "Did you know separation of church and state is a myth?"

Barton's historical revisionism begins with the Constitutional Convention of 1787. At one point the convention almost collapsed because of bickering between delegates. Knowing that the future of the whole American enterprise was endangered, Benjamin Franklin suggested that they humbly implore "the assistance of heaven." Interestingly enough, his request for prayer met opposition, and when it was brought to a vote—it failed! Thus the convention that wrote the U.S. Constitution engaged in less group prayer than does the General Conference picnic committee.

Here's David Barton's spin on the event: "Franklin's admonition—and the delegates' response to it—had been the turning point not only for the convention, but also for the future of the nation. . . . With their repentance came a desire to begin each morning of official government business with prayer."

One of Barton's favorite quotes to promote the "Christian nation" notion was credited to Benjamin Franklin: "Whoever shall introduce into the public affairs the principles of primitive Christianity will change the face of the world." Another favorite (attributed to James Madison) was "We have staked the future of all our political institutions upon the capacity of each and all of us to govern ourselves . . . according to the Ten Commandments." Nice quotes, and they could buttress Barton's revisionist history, except for one problem—they're bogus (and Barton was finally forced to admit it).

Barton's premise is simple: America was founded as a "Christian nation" and thus was never meant to separate church and state. It's also wrong.

Many Founders *were* Christians of some stripe, and Christianity unquestionably influenced their views of humanity, government, and morality. But that doesn't mean they founded a Christian nation in the sense that they wanted the government to establish the Christian faith or any Christian institutions. On the contrary, with European soil bloodstained from centuries of violence incited by the unity of church and state, the Founders purposely separated them—a fact that Barton and the Religious Right won't accept because they see separation as hostile to religion.

Of course, far from hurting religion, separation from government strengthens it. Unless, that is, the religion's so weak it needs government support—exactly what's behind the Christian Right's attempt at political supremacy.

In *The Great Controversy* Ellen White wrote that when the early church lost the power of the Spirit "she sought the support of the secular power" (p. 443) to control the consciousness of the people; the result was "the beast" (Rev. 13:1-7). Now the same principles are at work, this time in the formation of the "image of the beast" (verses 14, 15). Devoid of the Spirit, the politicized church is seeking secular power instead—but to do so it must first rewrite America's past.

Foucalt warned that the study of history is a disinterested quest not for truth, but for power. David Barton, at least in this case, proves him right.

꩜

The Persecuted?

If you're a Christian in America, you're subjected to vicious persecution, government hostility, and (in case you haven't noticed) a systematic oppression aimed at eradicating you and your religion.

If you haven't noticed, that's because you haven't accepted the Christian Right's line that the American church is the victim of persecution.

Jerry Falwell warns that "Bible-believing Christianity" has been "outlawed" in America. Pat Buchanan bemoans the "Christian-bashing" so prevalent in America today. Tim LaHaye warns about "the government-inspired persecution that is going on in America today in the name of the First Amendment."

The Rutherford Institute writes about "religious apartheid" against Christians. Chuck Colson says that Christians have become a "persecuted minority." Even James Dobson has warned: "I believe that Christian op-pression is just around the corner. I really believe that the level of anger rising out of the homosexual community primarily, but the whole human-istic movement that's out there . . . as they gain political power—and they got it now—they're going to continue to oppress us."

New Right lawyer Keith Fournier explains: "Day after day the news media brings us horrific reports from the Balkans, Africa, and other foreign countries of ethnic-based attacks all-too reminiscent of the infamous Holocaust. . . . And yet a similar insanity is being perpetrated before our eyes in our own country. But ethnic origin isn't the target. It's religion and those who embrace it."

And finally, from multimillionaire business executive, media mogul, television personality, Republican Party power broker, and former presi-dential candidate Pat Robertson: "Just like what Nazi Germany did to the Jews, so liberal America is now doing to evangelical Christians."

Now, maybe I'm missing something here, but are we, as Christians in the United States, persecuted? Even as Adventists, with beliefs that sepa-rate us from the "mainstream," are we being systematically oppressed by gays, persecuted by the government, or subjected to a Nazilike genocide, all on account of our faith?

Maybe you are, but I'm not (and no one else in my local church is either).

Of course, some bias against Christianity does exist, even in America, and some might even face religious harassment from family or employers, but bias isn't persecution any more than a Jewish joke is the Holocaust. And for these Christians—most of them wealthy, powerful, and influen-tial—to portray themselves as victims of persecution makes a mockery of those Christians in other lands who really are.

In my work I daily read heart-wrenching accounts of Christians in Asia, Africa, and the Middle East who—facing torture, jail, exile, even death for their faith—don't whine as much as Robertson, Colson, or Falwell do about "persecution."

Why this shameful propaganda? The answer's simple: what better way to shake Christians out of their political complacency than to convince them that they're victims? If the faithful can be persuaded that the wall of separa-tion of church and state is persecuting them, that laws forbidding govern-ment-sponsored prayer in school are persecuting them, that the arrest of abortion protesters is persecuting them, and that such movies as *The Last Temptation of Christ* are persecuting them, they will respond. They already do.

Years ago a girl involved in the Religious Right told me that although at one time she was skeptical about getting into politics, she changed her mind after being warned by her church that "the American government is planning to take our Bibles from us!"

Take our Bibles from us?

I don't blame the girl; I blame the church leaders who, using their massive media outlets, disseminate bogus stories about oppression and harassment in order to involve their followers in politics, while the hostile, anti-Christian government not only protects their right to spread these stories—but lets them do it tax-free!

Some persecution.

———※———

City of Boerne v. Flores

In June I went to Brazil; a week later, upon landing in Washington, D.C., I felt as though I had returned to a foreign country.

I'm talking about *City of Boerne v. Flores,* in which a 6-3 majority on the U.S. Supreme Court struck down the Religious Freedom Restoration Act (RFRA). In one fell swoop the free exercise of religion, for years accorded special constitutional protection (the idea being that one's relationship to God was so sacred, so personal, that government shouldn't be allowed to interfere except in extraordinary circumstances), now has less protection than "obscene and indecent" messages on the Internet.

The background is this: since the early 1960s the onus was on the government to show that any "substantial burden" it placed on the free exercise of religion was justified by the least restrictive means of furthering a compelling state interest. In other words, if a law—however incidentally and unintentionally—hampered someone's free exercise of religion, the government needed to prove that it was in the paramount interest of the state to forbid these religious practices; otherwise, exemptions were constitutionally mandated.

Then in 1990, with *Employment Division Department of Human Resources of Oregon v. Smith, the U.S. Supreme Court* decided instead that if a law wasn't written specifically to hinder a religious practice, but applied to everyone equally, then even if that law had the "incidental effect" of prohibiting free exercise, tough luck. If your legislature will grant you the exemption, fine; if not, well—"majority rules."

Now, if you're a Jew in New York or a Mormon in Utah, chances are the local politicians won't ruffle your religious feathers. If, though, you're an American Indian in New York, or a Seventh-day Adventist in Utah, or a member of any faith anywhere without enough voters to get your legislators' attention, then since *Smith,* if a law incidentally tramples on your religious freedom, you're in trouble, because the courts can no longer protect you.

In response Congress passed RFRA, which reinstated the pre-*Smith* "compelling state interest" test, which said the government had to give a good reason for restricting a person's free exercise.

Unfortunately, the constitutionality of RFRA was challenged, and before long the U.S. Supreme Court had to rule on a law written specifically to undo one of its own decisions (sort of like asking Joe Camel to judge antismoking regulations). And, as feared, the High Court in *Flores* ruled RFRA unconstitutional.

According to Section 5 of the Fourteenth Amendment to the Constitution, Congress is allowed to pass "appropriate legislation" to ensure that constitutionally guaranteed rights (such as free exercise) are enforced. In short, Congress can pass only laws that protect already existing constitutional rights; it can't legislate new ones.

Though the majority's argument in *Flores* dealt primarily with "the separation of powers" and the question of whether Congress overstepped its bounds with RFRA, the Court looked at this issue from the premise that *Smith* (which protects people only from laws that *intentionally* restrict their free exercise) was the correct way to interpret the free exercise clause. RFRA was voided, therefore, because from the narrow standard of *Smith* it created rights that weren't already there. Much of this decision, wrote Justice O'Connor in her dissent, "is premised on the assumption that *Smith* correctly interprets the free exercise clause. This is an assumption that I do not accept."

If, however, the majority believed that the pre-*Smith* (the "compelling state interest") test was the correct interpretation, then RFRA would not have created any new constitutional rights, but would have simply been "appropriate legislation" to ensure that the already existing right of free exercise (as understood pre-*Smith*) was enforced.

On an immediate and pragmatic level, *Flores* means that minority religions will have a harder time practicing certain tenets of their faith. And on a grander scale, though not the end of the world (no, it doesn't mean Sunday laws are imminent), the decision should warn us that religious freedoms are fragile.

By the way, what was I doing in Brazil when I first heard about *Flores?* Attending a world congress on—of all things—religious liberty.